the
LOST
TRIBES

the
LOST
TRIBES

History, Doctrine, Prophecies and Theories About Israel's Lost Ten Tribes

R. Clayton Brough

Published by
Horizon Publishers
A division of Cedar Fort Inc.
www.cedarfort.com

Horizon
Publishers

v. 9 January 2005

ISBN: 0-88290-441-8

Library of Congress Number: 79-89351

Horizon Publishers' Catalog and Order Number:
C1031

Printed and distributed
in the United States of America by

& Distributors, Incorporated

Address:
925 North Main Street
Springville, Utah 84663

Local Phone: (801) 489-4084
Toll Free: 1 (800) SKYBOOK
FAX: (800) 489-1097

E-mail: horizonp@burgoyne.com
Internet: http://www.horizonpublishersbooks.com

To

My Loving wife and helpmate

Ethel,

And to my children

Alison, Richard, Michael and Adam.

Acknowledgments

I would like to express sincere love and appreciation to R. Marshall Brough, my father, and an expert in logic. Prior to his passing away on September 8, 1979, he critically read the original manuscript as it came from my typewriter. Without his encouragement and suggestions this book might never have been completed.

Appreciation also is extended to Bishop Mark E. Eubank, President of *WeatherBank Inc.*, who reviewed the completed manuscript of this book prior to its submission to the publisher, and who made several helpful editorial suggestions; to Dr. Dale J. Stevens. Associate Professor of Geography at Brigham Young University. for his continued friendship and encouragement of my research and writing projects, and who offered a number of excellent suggestions as to the survey conducted on the topic of this book; to Dr. Laren R. Robison, Professor and Chairman of the Department of Agronomy at Brigham Young University, whose questions on this topic encouraged me to investigate sources of materials I had not originally investigated; to Patrick D. Blakely, a scholar of many languages, for his input into many of the topics covered in this book; and to B. Kelly Nielsen, geographer and cartographer for the Department of Geography at Brigham Young University, for his production of the two maps that are in this book.

Also, deep appreciation is expressed to Duane S. Crowther, President of *Horizon Publishers*, who expertly assisted this author by making editorial and organizational suggestions in reading this book for publication, and whose friendship and judgment I have come to greatly appreciate and respect.

And last but most important. I am eternally grateful to my lovely and loving wife, Ethel, who has unselfishly sustained, encouraged, and assisted me during my many hours of research, writing and revisions. And finally, I feel most grateful to my Lord Jesus Christ, for His kindness and assistance towards me throughout this research endeavor, and for His sustaining me in health and strength, alertness of mind, and inspiration of Spirit.

R. Clayton Brough

Contents

Introduction

This author wishes his readers to understand, from the very beginning, that he has not written this book for the purpose of determining the present abode of the Lost Ten Tribes of Israel, nor to put forth yet another theory as to their present whereabouts. Indeed, so many untenable theories have been proposed in the past that, in a way, the Lost Ten Tribes have been found and lost again so often that any new material written on the subject is now often looked upon only with distrust.

Therefore, wanting to avoid this possible attitude of skepticism, while sincerely wishing to enlarge the knowledge of the general membership of the Church upon this intriguing gospel subject, this author has written this book for two general purposes: *first*, to bring together into one encompassing work what scriptural and modern revelation has revealed to us about the history and prophetic destiny of the Lost Ten Tribes of Israel; and *second*, through a system of delicate arrangement and appropriate commentary, to strive to clarify and summarize the many statements of the various theories, beliefs, positions, opinions and/or outright speculations that early General Authorities of the Church and those Brethren in our own times have expressed about the present possible location of the Lost Ten Tribes.

Hence, this author will not introduce in this work any new theories as to the possible location of the Lost Ten Tribes today, but will only endeavor to objectively bring a good portion of "order and understanding" to a subject that many Latter-day Saints still feel is full of "conflicting and mysterious teachings." It is hoped that this book will achieve that goal.

In addition, the reader should be aware that this is not an official Church publication and that this writer is solely responsible for the manner in which documented material is presented within this book. It is appropriate that those who read this book seek inspiration from the Holy Ghost as to the truthfulness of the information contained herein.

R. Clayton Brough

One

The Early History
Of The
Twelve Tribes Of Israel

In order to appreciate and understand the Biblical and latter-day teachings and prophecies that deal with the Lost Ten Tribes of Israel, a brief account of the history and geography of the Twelve Tribes of Israel is first necessary. Therefore, this chapter shall undertake to accomplish this endeavor by using scriptural documentation and other generally accepted scholarly information, written in a concise and readable fashion.

Jacob and His Twelve Sons

In the Old Testament, Jacob, whom the Lord named "Israel," was the son of Isaac and grandson of Abraham. He was born about 1836 B.C.[1] in the land of Canaan (which was later called Palestine) and was the father of twelve sons: Reuben, Simeon, Levi, Judah, Issachar, and Zebulun (who were Jacob's sons by his first wife, Leah), Dan and Naphtali (Jacob's sons by Bilhah, the handmaiden of Rachel), Gad and Asher (Jacob's sons by Zilpah, Leah's handmaiden), and Joseph and Benjamin (Jacob's sons by Rachel, who was Jacob's second but most favored wife). (Gen. 29-30.)

Jacob was most faithful in magnifying his priesthood and patriarchal responsibilities, and as a result of this and his devotion to God, the Lord made the same covenants and promises to Jacob as He had made with Jacob's father, Isaac, and grandfather,

---

1. The chronology dates that appear in this chapter are taken from the "Chronological Tables" of the *Concise Bible Dictionary*, pp. 23-26. Although other individuals and a number of recent books have different birth and beginning dates for some of the people and events of the Old Testament, nevertheless, the relative time periods between biblical events in these modern works remain basically compatible with those of the *Concise Bible Dictionary*. For another chronological listing, see: *An Analysis of Old Testament Chronology in the Light of Modern Scripture & Scientific Research*, by Dale A. McAllister (Thesis, B Y.U., Provo, Utah, 1963. 119 pages).

Abraham. Regarding these covenants and promises which the Lord bestowed upon Jacob, let us first consider the promises of the Lord unto Abraham and his seed, the children of Israel:

> And the LORD said, Shall I hide from Abraham that thing which I do;
>
> Seeing that Abraham shall surely become a great and mighty nation, and *all the nations of the earth shall be blessed in him?* (Genesis 18:17-18.)

Abraham's willingness to offer up his son Isaac as a sacrificial offering, as he had been commanded, brought forth a confirmation of the covenant and an enlargement thereof:

> And the angel of the LORD called unto Abraham out of heaven the second time,
>
> And said, By myself have I sworn, saith the LORD, for because thou hast done this thing, and hast not withheld thy son, thine only son:
>
> That in blessing I will bless thee, and in multiplying I will multiply thy seed as the stars of the heaven, and as the sand which is upon the sea shore; and thy seed shall possess the gate of his enemies;
>
> And in thy seed shall all the nations of the earth be blessed; because thou hast obeyed my voice. (Genesis 22:15-18.)

Later, this same covenant and promise the Lord had made with Abraham was renewed with his son, Isaac:

> And there was a famine in the land, beside the first famine that was in the days of Abraham. And Isaac went unto Abimelech king of the Philistines unto Gerar.
>
> And the LORD appeared unto him, and said, Go not down into Egypt; dwell in the land which I shall tell thee of:
>
> Sojourn in this land, and I will be with thee, and will bless thee; for unto thee, and unto thy seed, 1 will give all these countries, and I will perform the oath which I sware unto Abraham thy father;
>
> And I will make thy seed to multiply as the stars of heaven, and will give unto thy seed all these countries; and *in thy seed shall all the nations of the earth be blessed;*
>
> Because that Abraham obeyed my voice, and kept my charge, my commandments, my statutes, and my laws. (Genesis 26:1-5.)

And likewise, the Lord made this same covenant with Jacob, the son of Isaac:

And Jacob went out from Beer-sheba, and went toward Haran.

And he lighted upon a certain place, and tarried there all night, because the sun was set; and he took of the stones of that place, and put them for his pillows, and lay down in that place to sleep.

And he dreamed, and behold a ladder set up on the earth, and the top of it reached to heaven: and behold the angels of God ascending and descending on it.

And, behold, the LORD stood above it, and said, I am the LORD God of Abraham thy father, and the God of Isaac: the land whereon thou liest, to thee will I give it, and to thy seed;

And thy seed shall be as the dust of the earth, and thou shalt spread abroad to the west, and to the east, and to the north, and to the south: and *in thee and in thy seed shall all the families of the earth be blessed.* (Genesis 28:10-14.)

In summary, the covenant and promises the Lord made with Abraham, Isaac, and Jacob were:

1. "Abraham shall surely become a great and mighty nation."
2. "I will give unto thee all these countries."
3. "I will multiply thy seed as the stars of the heavens, and as the sand, which is upon the seashore."
4. "And in thy seed shall all the nations of the earth be blessed."

With these wonderful promises that the Lord had given to the posterity of Abraham and Isaac, He gave to their posterity, through Jacob, a special name by which they would be known among all peoples, even the name of "Israel," or "Israelites," which name or designation has continued with them to this day. In fact, their God is referred to as the "God of Israel."

At the time Jacob wrestled with an angel at Peniel, the angel changed Jacob's name to Israel.

Regarding Jacob's new name, Elder Legrand Richards, an apostle, has written:

Jacob's new name, Israel, became the family name. The posterity of Abraham and Isaac, through Jacob came to be known variously as "Israel," "Children of Israel," "House of

Israel," "Tribes of Israel." Their descendants are known as "Israelites" to this day . . . .

A careful consideration of the 46th chapter of Genesis, naming the sons and daughters of Jacob and their families, will clearly establish the fact that all of the children of Jacob were called after his new name, "Israel," and were known as "Israelites." It should be emphasized that this designation applied to all the sons of Jacob, and not to the posterity of his son Judah only. Therefore, the fulfillment of the promises of the Lord unto Abraham, Isaac and Jacob, will not be realized through any one branch of the House of Israel, but through all of them.[2]

During the lifetime of Jacob, two very important events occurred to him and his twelve sons. The first of these two events was the selling of Jacob's son, Joseph, by his brothers to Midianite merchantmen, who then sold Joseph into Egypt in about 1728 B.C. In the circumstances which followed, Joseph had the opportunity of blessing his father's entire family with food during seven years of famine that occurred in the Middle East. This prompted his father to move his family and kindred, then numbering about 70 people, from Canaan into Egypt about 1706 B.C. There the "Israelites" grew and "multiplied exceedingly" for about 215 years. Their population reached a figure of possibly some two million inhabitants.[3] (Gen. 37-48)

The second well-known event, which occurred collectively to Jacob's sons, was the receiving of patriarchal blessings from their father, Jacob, who, when nearing his time of death, gave his twelve sons and two of the sons of Joseph, Ephraim and Manasseh, patriarchal blessings, which foretold what would happen to them and to their descendants.[4] (Gen. 48-49, *Inspired Version*). Through a careful study and consideration of the blessings of the Lord which were pronounced through Jacob, upon his twelve sons, it is evident that they were not to share equally in the promises of the Lord:

And Jacob called unto his sons, and said, Gather yourselves together, that I may tell you that which shall befall you in the last days.

---

2. Legrand Richards, *Israel Do You Know*, Deseret Book Company, S.L.C., Utah, 1954, pp. 6-8.

3. Anthony W. Ivins, "The Lost Tribes" (A personal letter on file at B.Y.U., #Mor, M238,2 Iv 51.) Early 1900's, pp. 2-4, 5-8. 15 total pages.

4. Bruce R. McConkie, *Mormon Doctrine*, Bookcraft Inc., S.L.C., Utah, 1966, 856 pages, p. 808.

Gather yourselves together, and hear, ye sons of Jacob; and hearken unto Israel your father.

Reuben, thou art my firstborn, my might, and the beginning of my strength, the excellency of dignity, and the excellency of power:

Unstable as water, thou shalt not excel; because thou wentest up to thy father's bed; then defiledst thou it: he went up to my couch.

Simeon and *Levi* are brethren; instruments of cruelty are in their habitations.

O my soul, come not thou into their secret; unto their assembly, mine honour, be not thou united: for in their anger they slew a man, and in their selfwill they digged down a wall.

Cursed be their anger, for it was fierce; and their wrath, for it was cruel: I will divide them in Jacob, and scatter them in Israel.

Judah, thou art he whom thy brethren shall praise: thy hand shall be in the neck of thine enemies; thy father's children shall bow down before thee.

Judah is a lion's whelp: from the prey, my son, thou art gone up: he stooped down, he couched as a lion, and as an old lion; who shall rouse him up?

The sceptre shall not depart from Judah, nor a lawgiver from between his feet, until Shiloh come; and unto him shall the gathering of the people be.

Binding his foal unto the vine, and his ass's colt unto the choice vine; he washed his garments in wine, and his clothes in the blood of grapes:

His eyes shall be red with wine, and his teeth white with milk.

Zebulun shall dwell at the haven of the sea; and he shall be for an haven of ships; and his border shall be unto Zidon.

Issachar is a strong ass couching down between two burdens:

And he saw that rest was good, and the land that it was pleasant; and bowed his shoulder to bear, and became a servant unto tribute.

Dan shall judge his people, as one of the tribes of Israel.

Dan shall be a serpent by the way, an adder in the path, that biteth the horse heels, so that his rider shall fall backward.

I have waited for thy salvation, O Lord.

Gad, a troop shall overcome him: but he shall overcome at the last.

Out of *Asher* his bread shall be fat, and he shall yield royal dainties.

Naphtali is a hind let loose: he giveth goodly words.

Joseph is a fruitful bough, even a fruitful bough by a well; whose branches run over the wall:

The archers have sorely grieved him, and shot at him, and hated him:

But his bow abode in strength, and the arms of his hands were made strong by the hands of the mighty God of Jacob; (from thence is the shepherd, the stone of Israel:)

Even by the God of thy father, who shall help thee; and by the Almighty, who shall bless thee with blessings of heaven above, blessings of the deep that lieth under, blessings of the breasts, and of the womb:

The blessings of thy father have prevailed above the blessings of my progenitors unto the utmost bound of the everlasting hills: they shall be on the head of Joseph, and on the crown of the head of him that was separate from his brethren.

Benjamin shall ravin as a wolf: in the morning he shall devour the prey, and at night he shall divide the spoil.

All these are the twelve tribes of Israel: and this is it that their father spake unto them, and blessed them; every one according to his blessing he blessed them. (Genesis 49:1-28. See Deuteronomy, Chapter 33, for a record of the blessings of Moses upon the twelve sons of Jacob.)

As is probably evident to the reader, the above blessings given to Judah and Joseph were choice above the blessings pronounced upon their brothers.

The Twelve Tribes in the Land of Canaan

In about 1491 B.C., approximately 215 years after Jacob had taken his family into Egypt, the children of Israel who were the descendants of Jacob's twelve sons, were collectively led out of Egypt by Moses and sojourned in the wilderness for 40 years. Concerning the number of Israelites who exited Egypt during the early part of this century, Elder Anthony W. Ivins, an Apostle, has commented:

. . . At the time of the exodus (of the Israelites from Egypt under Moses,) six-hundred and three-thousand five-hundred men went out with Moses who were twenty years old and upwards, and capable of bearing arms. (Numbers 1:45)

Counting four persons for each one capable of bearing arms, and we have more than two million people who went out from Egypt, which makes clear the fact that those who entered Palestine forty years later, and under the leadership of Joshua took possession of the promised land, were a numerous people.[5]

Under the direction of the Prophet Joshua, who succeeded Moses, the Israelite people, through the divine assistance of the Lord, conquered the land of Canaan (later called "Palestine") and established themselves as the Twelve Tribes of Israel (in about 1451 B.C.), all within a geographical area about one-eighth of the size of Utah. (See *Map A,* "The Establishment of the Twelve Tribes of Israel in the Land of Canaan," page 22.)

Regarding the partitioning of the land of Canaan into geographical entities governed by the Twelve Tribes of Israel, and the tribes subsequent territorial expansions, Elder Ivins has further stated:

Palestine, (formerly "Canaan) at the time it was partitioned among the twelve tribes of Israel, contained an area of about 10,000 square miles . . . . It was upon this comparatively small tract of land that the twelve tribes received their allotted heritage.

The tribe of Dan received their allotment in the extreme north of Palestine, while Simeon and Judah occupied the south. A careful reading of the Scriptures shows that the tribes were indiscriminately mixed together, an example of this being the statement that while the tribe of Dan was established in the extreme north, a part of the tribe was in the extreme south with Simeon and Judah. Benjamin also remained with Judah.

During a period of 454 years, a greater period than their sojourn in Egypt, the twelve tribes lived under one government, were subject to one reigning line of kings, transacted their business as one people, and fought their battles as one nation.

It cannot be doubted that during this period they had greatly increased in numbers, that intermarriage was of common occurrence, and tribes consequently almost indiscriminately mixed together, but still retaining their tribal distinction.

Nor was it long after the possession of Palestine that the people began to reach out and seek greater opportunities for expansion.

Forty years after their establishment in Palestine, the tribe of Dan, finding that the "coast of their inheritance went out too

---

5. Anthony W. Ivins, *op. cit.,* p. 2.

little for them," went up to fight against Le-shem, and took it, and smote it with the edge of the sword, and possessed it, and dwelt therein, and called it Le-shem Dan, after the name of Dan, their father (Joshua 19:47; Judges, Chapter 18.)

Under King Solomon Israel realized her Golden Age. Tribute was collected from all surrounding nations. Adoniram was his collector of taxes. (Andoniram and Adoram were the same person). He also served in this capacity under his son Rehoboam after the latter succeeded to the throne.

At Zaragoza, in Spain, there is a tombstone with the following inscription: "This is the tomb of Adoniram, the servant of King Solomon, who came to collect tribute and died here."

Now turn to your Bible, 1 Kings 4:6 and 12:18. It shows that this man, Adoniram (or Adoram, who is the same person) was sent into Spain to collect tribute, and all Israel rose up and stoned him to death.

"Therefore Rehoboam made speed to get him up to his chariot to flee to Jerusalem."

This makes plain the fact that three hundred years before the Ten Tribes were carried into captivity by Shalmanezer, Israel had extended its empire as far as Spain. (Elder Ivins then continues with a review of historical documents that suggest and indicate that possibly the tribe of Dan had, in one way or another, extended its influence and trade to "the (then known) British Isles and the Scandinavian countries of Europe" prior to the time the Ten Tribes were taken into captivity by King Shalmanezer of the Assyrians.)[6]

The Kingdom of Judah and the Kingdom of Israel

After Joshua's twenty-two-year reign over the Twelve Tribes, Israel was unitedly governed by Judges for 334 years and by three Kings: Saul, David, and Solomon, for another 120 years. Then, after the death of Solomon in 975 B.C., the Twelve Tribes of Israel divided into two Kingdoms: the Kingdom of Judah and the Kingdom of Israel.

The Kingdom of Judah was comprised of the tribe of Judah and most of the tribe of Benjamin, plus many of the descendants of Levi and a few individuals from almost all of the other tribes (since Judah controlled the city of Jerusalem and those individuals who

---

6. *Ibid.*

were merchants, traders, etc., undoubtedly lived in Jerusalem among the tribe of Judah[7]). The descendants of the people of the Kingdom of Judah later became known as the "Jews."

The Kingdom of Israel (or the "Kingdom of Ephraim" as it was sometimes called because Ephraim was the most prominent tribe) was comprised of the other "ten tribes" of Israel: Reuben, Simeon, Issachar, Zebulun, Dan, Naphtali, Gad, Asher, Ephraim, and Manasseh. The reason why the tribe of Joseph and Levi are not specifically named among the Ten Tribes of the Kingdom of Israel, and Ephraim and Manassah are, is because Joseph received a double portion through his two sons, Ephraim and Manasseh, while Levi's inheritance was the priesthood; for the scriptures tell us:

> Behold, they are mine, and the God of my fathers shall bless them; even as Reuben and Simeon they shall be blessed, for they are mine; wherefore they shall be called after my name. (Therefore they were called Israel.)
>
> And thy issue which thou begettest after them, shall be thine, and shall be called after the name of their brethren in their inheritance, in the tribes; therefore they were called the tribes of Manasseh and of Ephraim. (Gen. 48:5-6, *Inspired Version.*)

Thus Joseph inherited a double portion of Israel, and because the Lord chose the Levites to be his ministers (Ex. 32:25-29; Num. 8) an inheritance was given to both Ephraim and Manasseh in the promised land. (Num.1; Josh.13:14, 33; 14:1-5.)

Concerning the division of Israel after 975 B.C. into its two main kingdoms, Elder Bruce R. McConkie has stated:

> Beginning with the reign of Saul (about 1095 B.C.), Israel became a kingdom and so continued until her final destruction as a nation. After the death of Solomon (about 975 B.C.), however, the kingdom was divided. The tribes of Judah and part of the tribe of Benjamin, maintaining their allegiance and following Rehoboam, son of Solomon, became known as the Kingdom of Judah; the rest of the Israelites, commonly called the Ten tribes, followed Jeroboam and were known as the Kingdom of Israel, or sometimes as the Kingdom of Ephraim, after their most prominent tribe.[8]

---

7.   Duane S. Crowther, *Prophets & Prophecies of the Old Testament*, Horizon Publishers, Bountiful. Utah. 1966, pp. 38-39.

8. Bruce R. McConkie, op. cit., p. 418.

And Elder Anthony W. Ivins has similarly expressed:

It was after the death of King Solomon and the succession
of his son, Rehoboam, to the throne that the Ten Tribes revolted, separated from Judah, and parts of the other tribes who
remained with Rehoboam, selected Jerohoam, the son of Nebat
of the tribe of Ephraim to be their king, and established their
capital city at Shechem, but later removing to Samaria, which
became the principal city of Israel. (1 Kings 12.)

The house of Israel was thus divided into two kingdoms,
one governed by the house of Judah. and the other by the house
of Ephraim. The two kingdoms continued to exist for a period of
about 250 years. . . .[9]

Also, in reference to the Ten Tribes of Israel being identified collectively as (the Kingdom of) Ephraim (e.g.: the Kingdom of Israel),
Elder Ivins has further commented:

The heirship over all the house of Israel, originally conferred upon Judah, was taken from him and given to Ephraim,
as the following shows: "And thine house, and thy Kingdom
shall be established for ever before thee, thy throne shall be
established for ever." (2 Samuel 7:16.)

This promise held good until the reign of Solomon, the son
of David, at which time the ten tribes were given to the house
of Ephraim through Jeroboam, the son of Nebat, who was the
first king of Israel.

Because of the transgression of Solomon the Lord revoked
the promise made to David, as follows: "And he said to
Jeroboam take ten pieces, for thus saith the LORD, the God of
Israel, Behold, I will rend the kingdom out of the hand of
Solomon, and will give ten tribes to thee." (Jeroboam, the son of
Nebat, of the tribe of Ephraim) (1 Kings 11:31.)

After the death of Solomon this promise was realized when
the ten tribes revolted, leaving Rehoboam to reign over the house
of Judah and those who remained with him.

From that time the Israelitish people have been referred to
collectively as Judah and Ephraim.

"The head of Ephraim is Samaria." Samaria was the capital
city of the ten tribes. (Isaiah 7:9).

---

9. Ivins, *op. cit.*, p. 8.

"The envy also of Ephraim shall depart, and the adversaries of Judah shall be cut off. Ephraim shall not envy Judah, and Judah shall not vex Ephraim." (Isaiah 11:13.)

There are many other passages of scripture in which the ten tribes collectively are referred to as Ephraim, while those who remained with Judah are referred to as Judah.

This heirship to stand at the head of the Israelitish people was sealed upon Ephraim at the time when Jacob laid his hands upon the younger son of Joseph, and conferred upon him the heirship to the blessings pronounced upon the head of his father. (Gen. 49:22-28)

In modern revelation Ephraim is referred to as representing the ten tribes.

"And with Moroni, whom I have sent unto you to reveal the Book of Mormon, containing the fulness of my everlasting gospel, to whom I have committed the keys of the record of the stick of Ephraim. (*Doctrine and Covenants,* Sec. 27: verse 5).

"And it was told the house of David, saying: Syria is confederate with Ephraim." (*Book of Mormon,* p 79 verse 2.) "And all people shall know, even Ephraim, and the inhabitants of Samaria." "The envy of Ephraim also shall depart, and the adversaries of Judah shall be cut off; Ephraim shall not envy Judah, and Judah shall not vex Ephraim." (*Book of Mormon,* p 82, verse 9; and p. 85, verse 13.)[10]

In 1982, John A. Tvedtnes, a doctoral candidate in Egyptian and Semitic languages, wrote an article entitled "The 'Other Tribes', Which Are They?", that appeared in the *Ensign* (LDS Church, January, 1982, pp. 31-32). In his article, Brother Tvedtnes stated:

"We count ten 'lost' tribes of the northern kingdom of Israel by remembering that the tribe of Joseph was divided into three land and people elements for the purpose of land inheritance—Ephraim and the two subdivisions of Manasseh. Hence, the 'ten lost tribes' are ten lost land groups and are accounted for as follows: Reuben, Ephraim, Issachar, Naphtali, Gad, Asher, Dan, Half-tribe of Manasseh, Zebulun, and Half-tribe of Manasseh (Machir)."

---

10. Ivins, *op. cit.,* pp. 13-14.

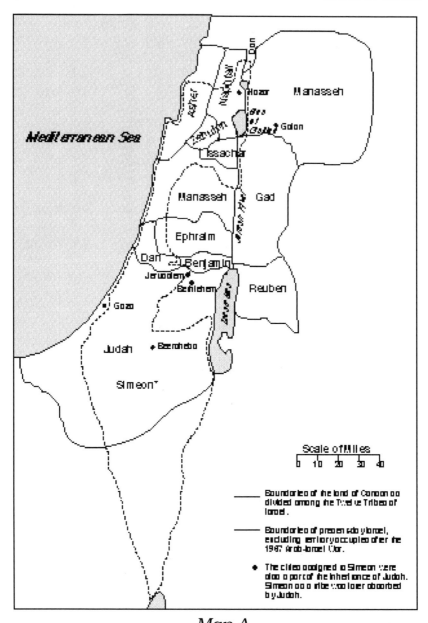

Map A
**The Establishment of the Twelve Tribes of Israel
in the Land of Canaan**

Two

The Historical Geography Of The Lost Ten Tribes Of Israel

The Assyrian Captivity of the Ten Tribes

About 254 years after the separation of the Kingdom of Israel from the Kingdom of Judah, King Shalmaneser V, King of the Assyrians, led his army in an invasion of the northern portion of the land of Palestine.[1] This was in about 723 B.C., during the ninth year of the reign of King Joshea (2 Kings 17:6), the last king to rule over the ten tribes comprising the Kingdom of Israel.

During the invasion, the Assyrians placed the major Israelite city of Samaria under siege for three years. At the end of the three-year siege, in about 721 B.C., the Assyrians "conquered Samaria" and the other areas of northern Palestine. They initially took "into captivity 27,290" Israelites, carrying them off to the Assyrian districts of Halah and Habor near the river Gozan (a tributary of the river Euphrates), and to various other cities of the Medes in the Assyrian-controlled country of Media, a region located just east of the Tigris and Euphrates rivers. (2 Kings 17:5-6).[2] Later, the Assyrian "evacuation of the Israelites" from Palestine to Assyria continued until this northern region of Palestine was "almost denuded of Israelite population."[3] Regarding this event, W. Cleon Skousen, former professor of ancient scripture at Brigham Young University, has written:

> Meanwhile, the original Israelite inhabitants of Samaria had been dragged off to Assyria and consigned to the same cities

---

1. 2 Kings 17:5-6. Bruce R. McConkie, *op. cit.*, pp. 418-419. W. Cleon Skousen, *Fourth Thousand Years*. Bookcraft, S.L.C., Utah, 1966, pp. 496-501. (Skousen quotes Kraeling, Rand McNally *Bible Atlas*, pp. 297-298.)

2. 2 Kings 17:56. *Concise Bible Dictionary, op. cit.*, p. 48. W. Cleon Skousen. *op. cit.*, pp. 496-501.

3. W. Cleon Skousen, *op. cit.*, pp. 496-501.

where the earlier captives of Israel had been settled. It will be recalled that some ten years earlier Tiglath-pileser III had captured the Israelites around Galilee as well as those in Trans-Jordan and had compelled them to travel by forced marches to "Halah, and Habor, and Hara, and to the river Gozan." When Sargon II [who took over the throne of Assyria when King Shalmaneser V died by assassination while laying siege to Samaria] conquered Samaria and the rest of Israel he pushed the captives together and marched them off to the same places. As the scripture says, "In the ninth year of Hoshea, the king of Assyria [Sargon II] took Samaria, and carried Israel away into Assyria, and placed them in Halah and Habor by the river of Gozan, and in the cities of the Medes." [2 Kings 17:6]

Dr. Emil G. Kraeling makes this comment concerning the region where the Ten Tribes were taken:

"According to the Biblical account, he [Sargon II] settled them in Halah on the Habor, the river of Gozan, and in the cities of the Medes. Halah lay northeast of Nineveh, which city at a slightly later day had a gate named the 'gate of the land of Halah (Halahhu). Since there is reason to believe that the city lay between Nineveh and Sargon's new capital (Khorsabad), the large mound of Tell 'Abassiyeh has been nominated for it. Excavations there might give us traces of the ten lost tribes.

"The Habor region, which is mentioned next is that of the river which to this day bears the same name, Khabur, and enters the Euphrates from the north. If this is the river described as 'the river of Gozan,' it has become more vivid through the rediscovery of the ancient city of Gozan. This City (Guzana in the cuneiform texts) is at Tell Halaf where interesting finds were made in excavations carried on by Baron M. von Oppenheim in 1911-13. It lay near Ras el 'Ain at the source of the Khabur River . . . . Other Israelites were taken much farther to the northeast, to 'the cities of the Medes.' These people (the Medes) had only recently entered the world picture, and Agbatana (Ecbatana), today called Hamadan, was their capital. However, the reference to 'cities of the Medes' remains vague. Cities under Assyrian control must be meant, and these will hardly have been very far to the north. As the Medes later inherited northern Mesopotamia, the phrase may refer to cities around the *Khabur* sources." [Kraeling, Rand McNally *Bible Atlas,* pp. 297-298.][4]

Some have questioned why the Lord permitted the Ten Tribes to be taken captive by the Assyrians. The reason is that the Israelite people had become so engrossed in idolatry and wickedness that they were ripe for destruction, and needed to be chastised, humbled, and again brought into a remembrance of the Lord (2 Kings 17:1-18). This is clarified in the following commentary:

> Jeroboam, the first king of the Northern Kingdom, deliberately encouraged the people into idolatry. Because he feared the people would go to Jerusalem to worship at the temple and decide to remain there, he built a golden calf at Bethel and one at Dan and told his people they were the gods that brought them out of Egypt (1 Kings 12:25-33). It seems that the Israelites needed little encouragement and were soon steeped in idolatry. Following Jeroboam came a long list of kings, none of whom were righteous men, and each followed the idolatrous practices of Jeroboam. The Lord was grieved at this rebellion against him and the covenant. Therefore he sent many prophets to the kingdom of Israel to cry repentance and warn of impending destruction and captivity. The people rejected each prophet in turn and continued in their wickedness. Political, religious, and individual corruption was rampant.[5]

The Ten Tribes Escape Assyrian Captivity and Travel Northward

After a stay of some years as captives in Assyria (from about 720 to before 610 B.C.),[6] the Ten Tribes of Israel eventually managed to escape from their Assyrian captors. Apparently the Lord assisted them in this endeavor,[7] since during the course of their Assyrian bondage they had warranted His help by humbling themselves to the extent of finally receiving a strong desire to "leave the multitude of the heathen, and go forth unto a further country where never

---

4. *Ibid.*

5. Lesson Manual: *Seminary Course of Study, Old Testament Student Manual,* The Church of Jesus Christ of Latter-day Saints. Department of Seminaries & Institutes of Religion, Salt Lake City, Utah, 1967, p. 54.

6. The Assyrian Empire was effectively destroyed by 610 A.D.

7. 3 Nephi 21:26.

man dwelt, that they might there keep their statutes [that the Lord had initially given them], which they never kept in their own land [of Palestine]." (2 Esdras 13:41-42, *Apocrypha*.)

Upon leaving the grasp of the Assyrians (sometime prior to 610 B.C.), the Ten Tribes, who may have then increased to a population of "perhaps not exceeding a hundred thousand people,"[8] first moved in a southerly direction towards Palestine, possibly to deceive their former captors. However, after crossing the Euphrates river they turned their journey northward and later traveled "through" an unknown geographical region called "Arsareth" [or Ararath].[9] Concerning this movement of the Ten Tribes from Assyria, and their later journey through the region of Arsareth, the Prophet Esdras, in the *Apocrypha*,[10] has given us the following account:

> Those are the Ten Tribes which were carried away captives out of their own land in the time of Oseas the king who Salmaneser the king of Assyrians took captive and crossed them beyond the river; so were they brought into another land.
>
> But they took this counsel to themselves, that they would leave the multitude of the heathen, and go forth unto a further country where never man dwelt.
>
> That they might there keep their statutes, which they never kept in their own land.
>
> And they entered in at the narrow passages of the River Euphrates.
>
> For the Most High then showed them signs, and stayed the springs of the flood till they were passed over.
>
> For through the country there was great journey, even of a year and a half, and the same region is called Arsareth.

---

8. Earnest L. Whitehead, *The House of Israel*, Zion Printing & Publishing Company, Independence, Missouri, 1947, p. 88. George Reynolds, *Are We of Israel?*, Deseret News Press, S.L.C., Utah, 1879. (Copyright by: Joseph F. Smith, for the Deseret Sunday School Union.), pp. 25-27.

9. In Hebrew the term "Arsareth" means "another land." George Reynolds, *op. cit.*, pp. 26-27. 2 Esdras 13:40-47 (*Apocrypha*).

10. 2 Esdras 13:40-47. It should be remembered that Joseph Smith was told by the Lord not to revise the Apocrypha while he was working on the rest of the translation of the Bible. The Lord explained that there were "many things contained therein that are true, and it is mostly translated correctly," but there were also "many things contained therein that are not true. which are interpolations by the hands of men." (D&C 91:1-6) Which of these two headings this particular account in Esdras falls under is perhaps questionable, although the much use and quotation of these passages by many of the General Authorities tends to add authoritative support for its credibility.

Then dwelt they there until the latter time, and when they come forth again.

The Most High shall hold still the spring of the river again that they may go through; therefore sawest thou the multitude peaceable. (2 Esdras 13:40-47)

Commenting on this passage of Apocryphal scripture Elder George Reynolds, one of the early Seven Presidents of the First Quorum of Seventy, wrote in 1879 the following geographical review,[11] which the church, through its teachings and instructional manuals and from statements by its General Authorities and other biblical scholars, has continually proposed as the possible, if not probable route that the Ten Tribes initially traveled after their escape from Assyrian bondage:[12]

They [the ten tribes] determined to go to a country where man never dwelt, that they might be free from all contaminating influences. That country could only be found in the north. Southern Asia was already the seat of a comparatively ancient civilization. Egypt flourished in northern Africa, and southern Europe was rapidly filling with the future rulers of the world. They had, therefore, no choice but to turn their faces northward. The first portion of their journey was not however north; according to the account of Esdras, they appear to have at first moved in the direction of their old homes, and it is possible that they originally started with the intention of returning thereto, or probably in order to deceive the Assyrians they started as if to return to Canaan, and when they had crossed the Euphrates, and were out of danger from the hosts of the Medes and Persians, then they turned their journeying feet toward the polar star. Esdras states that they entered in at the narrow passages of the River Euphrates, the Lord staying the springs of the flood until they were passed over. The point on the River Euphrates at which they crossed would necessarily be in its upper portion, as lower down would be too far south for their purpose.

The upper course of the Euphrates lies among lofty mountains and near the village of Pastash, it plunges through a gorge formed by precipes more than a thousand feet in height and so narrow that it is bridged at the top; it shortly afterward enters the plains of Mesopotamia. How accurately this portion of the

---

11. George Reynolds. *op. cit.,* pp. 25-27.

12 Examples: Lesson Manual, *op. cit.,* pp. 78-79; *Bruce R. McConkie, op. cit.,* pp. 418-419, 457-458; George Reynolds, *op. cit.,* pp. 25-27.

river answers the description of Esdras of the narrows, where the Israelites crossed!

From the Euphrates the wandering host could take but one course in their journey northward, and that was along the back or eastern shore of the Black Sea. All other roads were impassable to them, as the Caucasian range of mountains with only two or three passes throughout its whole extent, ran as a lofty barrier from the Black to the Caspian Sea. To go east would take them back to Media, and a westward journey would carry them through Asia Minor to the coasts of the Mediterranean. Skirting along the Black Sea, they would pass the Caucasian range, cross the Kuban River, be prevented by the Sea of Azof from turning westward and would soon reach the present home of the Don Cossaks [in southwestern Russia].[13]

The Ten Tribes Travel Northwaro Through Arsareth ano Are Lost to Mankino

After the Ten Tribes had "entered in at the narrow passage of the River Euphrates,"[14] and possibly traveled around the westward side of the Caucasus Mountain Range in southwestern Russia,[15] they then proceeded in a more or less northerly direction through an unknown region that the Prophet Esdras called "Arsareth."[16] Whether this "region" of "Arsareth" is or is not identical to, part of, or encompassed in the geographical area referred to by the Prophets Jeremiah, Zechariah, and Joseph Smith, as "the land of the north" and/or "the north country(ies)" (which the scriptures indicate is the location that the Ten Tribes "shall come" from in the last days),[17] has not yet been revealed. Nevertheless, the term "Arsareth" has been used to identify the region that the Ten Tribes traveled "through" for approximately "a year and a half" during

13. George Reynolds, *op. cit.*, pp. 25-27.

14. 2 Esdras 13:43.

15. George Reynolds, *op. cit.*, pp. 26-27.

16. 2 Esdras 13:45.

17. The Prophet Jeremiah calls the location "the north country" (Jer 23:7-8; 31:8-9). Zechariah calls it "the land of the north" (Zech. 2:6), and Joseph Smith calls it both the land of the north" and/or "the north countries" (D&C 110:11; 133:26) It is interesting to note that Jeremiah uses both the terms "country" and "countries" in prophesying of the return of the House of Israel in the last days: "But the Lord liveth, which   brought up and which led the seed of the house of Israel out of the north country, and from all countries whither I had driven them: and they shall dwell in their own land" (Jer. 23:8).

their journey northward.[18] (See *Map B*, "The Possible Route of the Ten Tribes of Israel: Covering Their Journey From Palestine to Arsareth," page 36.)

As the possible "tens of thousands" of Israelites of the Ten Tribes traveled northward,[19] they undoubtedly passed through lands having few if any inhabitants.[20] Because of this and their expressed desire to "go forth into a further country, where never mankind dwelt," the Lord has since withheld the knowledge of their exact northward migration route and of their present location from the rest of mankind.[21] For as the scriptures indicate, though the Ten Tribes have never been lost to the Lord, they have become "lost from the knowledge" of the rest of mankind. Therefore the appropriate title: the "Lost Ten Tribes of Israel" (3 Nephi 15:15-20; 1 Nephi 22:4; 3 Nephi 17:4: D&C 110:11; 2 Nephi 29:13).

The Present Conditions of the Lost Ten Tribes

As the Lost Ten Tribes made their way northward through the unknown region of "Arsareth," they were "led by prophets and inspired leaders" who "were guided by the spirit of revelation, kept the law of Moses, and carried with them the statutes and judgments which the Lord had given them in ages past."[22] Indeed, the spirit of the Lord continually watched over the Lost Ten Tribes of Israel and guided them throughout their journey northward.[23]

In regard to other spiritual events that later transpired among the Lost Ten Tribes, such as the Lord personally visiting them following his ministry to the Nephites on the American continent, their being taught the Gospel, and their creating and maintaining volumes of scripture, Elder Bruce R. McConkie has written:

> In their northward journeyings they were led by prophets and inspired leaders. They had their Moses and their Lehi, were guided by the spirit of revelation, kept the law of Moses, and carried with them the statutes and judgements which the Lord had given them in ages past. They were still a distinct people many hundreds of years later, for the resurrected Lord visited and ministered among them following his ministry on this continent among the Nephites. (3 Nephi 16:1-4; 17:4) Obviously he taught

18. 2 Esdras 13:45. George Reynolds, *op. cit.*, pp. 26-27.
19. Earnest L. Whitehead, *op. cit.*, p. 88. George Reynolds, *op. cit.*, pp. 25-27.
20. George Reynolds, *op. cit.*, pp. 25-27.
21. Bruce R. McConkie. *op cit.*, pp. 457-458.
22. *Ibid.*
23. *Ibid.* Jer. 23:7-8; 16:14-15.

them in the same way and gave them the same truths which he gave his followers in Jerusalem and on the American continent; and obviously they recorded his teachings, thus creating volumes of scripture comparable to the Bible and Book of Mormon. (2 Nephi 29:12-14.)[24]

Following our Lord's resurrection and personal visit to the peoples of the Lost Ten Tribes of Israel, our Savior also assigned one of his chosen Apostles, John the Revelator, who is presently a "translated being,"[25] to watch over the Lost Ten Tribes and to assist them in preparing for their future return from "the land of the north" to the "New Jerusalem" (here on the American continent) in the last days.[26]

For example, in 1831, the Prophet Joseph Smith said in Kirkland, Ohio, that "John the Revelator" was then among "the ten tribes of Israel . . . . to prepare them for their return" in the last days.[27] Elder Franklin D. Richards, an apostle, similarly stated in 1884 that "the Apostle John" was specifically and presently looking after the Lost Ten Tribes, preparing them to "come to Zion and receive their crowns at the hands of their brethren of Ephraim."[28]

Thus it is that the Lost Ten Tribes of Israel, wherever they may be, are presently being led, taught, and prepared in the Gospel by chosen servants of the Lord, just as we in the Church today are likewise being instructed by living modern-day Prophets, Seers, and Revelators.

Not All the Israelites Who Traveled Northward Remained With the Lost Ten Tribes

Since the time of the Prophet Joseph Smith, and up through our own day and period, nearly every General Authority of the Church who has ever spoken or written upon the subject of the Lost Ten Tribes of Israel has concurred that at least a "sufficient number" or "large portion" of the Lost Ten Tribes are today "united together" as

24. Bruce R. McConkie, op. cit., pp. 457-458.

25. D & C 110:11. R. Clayton Brough, They Who Tarry, Horizon Publishers, Bountiful. Utah, 1976, pp. 37-43.

26. R Clayton Brough, op. cit., p. 43.

27. Joseph Fielding Smith, Essentials in Church History, Deseret Book Company, Salt Lake City, Utah, 1969, p. 126. (Statement by the Prophet Joseph Smith.)

28. Franklin D. Richards, Journal of Discourses, Vol. 25, p. 237.

"one body" or "one group" of people, who shall at sometime during these Last Days return from the "land of the north" and/or "the north country."[29] In fact, so unified are the Brethren of the Church upon this one teaching that this author, after spending two years of researching through a wide spectrum of Latter-day Saint literature, could only find one General Authority who even implied as a "possibility" that a sufficient number or large portion of the Lost Ten Tribes *might not* now be as one united group of people. This was Elder Brigham H. Roberts, one of the early First Seven Presidents of the Quorum of Seventy, who in 1912, expressed among his several other "opinions" as to where the Ten Tribes might possibly be located, that "it would have been quite possible for God to scatter and to lose the Ten Tribes of Israel among the nations of the earth."[30]

The fact that with near or total unanimity the General Authorities of the Church have consistently stated that a sufficient number or large portion of the Lost Ten Tribes are still united today as one body or group of people, strongly supports the recommendation that it would be well for us as Latter-day Saints not to ignore or dismiss this significant teaching. The following three quotations, the first by Elder Parley P. Pratt, an Apostle, the second by Elder Orson F. Whitney, an Apostle, and the third by President Joseph Fielding Smith, serve as appropriate examples of the many similar statements of other General Authorities relative to this teaching:

Parley P. Pratt:

The Jews are called dispersed because they are scattered among the nations; but the Ten Tribes are called outcasts

---

29. For example: James E. Talmage, *Articles of Faith*, pp. 339-341; Joseph Fielding Smith, *The Way to Perfection*, p. 130; Parley P. Pratt, *Voice of Warning*, pp. 30-31; Orson F. Whitney, *Saturday Night Thoughts*, p. 174; LeGrand Richards, *A Marvelous Work & Wonder*, pp. 218-219. (See also Chapter 3 of this book and the selected bibliography in this book.)

30. Brigham H. Roberts, *Defense of the Faith & the Saints*, Deseret News, Salt Lake City, Utah, 1912, Vol. 2, pp. 478-480. Note: Elder Anthony W. Ivins is sometimes quoted as maintaining this possible viewpoint. However, Elder Ivins only stated that he believed "the great majority" of the Anglo Saxon people of Europe are people descended from the ten tribes, not that the ten tribes could be totally accounted for among the present day Eurasian people. In fact, after making the preceding remark, Elder Ivins added: "I have not at any time said that there might not be representatives of the ten tribes hidden away of whose existence we have no knowledge." (Anthony W. Ivins, "The Lost Tribes," *op. cit.*, pp. 14-15.)

because they are cast out from the knowledge of the nations into a land by themselves.[31]

Orson F. Whitney:

If this be true [that the Ten Tribes are totally scattered among the Europeans] and those tribes were not intact totally at the time Joseph and Oliver received the keys of the gathering, why did they make so pointed a reference to the leading of the Ten Tribes from the land of the North? . . .What need to particularize as to the Ten Tribes, if they were no longer a distinct people? And why do our Articles of Faith give them a special mention? [32]

Joseph Fielding Smith:

The Ten Tribes were taken by force out of the land the Lord gave them. Many of them mixed with the peoples among whom they were scattered. A large portion, however, departed in one body into the north and disappeared from the rest of the world. Where they went and where they are we do not know. That they are intact we must believe, else how shall the scripture be fulfilled? There are too many prophecies concerning them and their return as a body for us to ignore the fact.[33]

As a consequence of the teaching by the General Authorities, that at least a sufficient number or large portion of the Lost Ten Tribes are still united today as one body or group of people, who sometime in these Last Days shall return "from the land of the north," some Latter-day Saints have raised the question: "Then why are there members of the Church today in Eurasia, America, and other parts of the world, whose patriarchal blessings inform them that they are from Ephraim, Manesseh, or once in a great while from another tribe which was among the Lost Ten Tribes of Israel?"

In response to this question, Elder George Reynolds, whose following statement has often been quoted by other General Authorities as an appropriate answer, has stated that as the Ten Tribes traveled northward and eventually became "lost" to mankind, that some of [the] "backsliding" Israelites "rebelled,

31. Parley P. Pratt, *A Voice of Warning and Instruction to All People*, Deseret News Publishing Company, Salt Lake City, Utah, 1893 (13th Edition), 258 pages; Brigham H. Roberts, *Defense of the Faith And The Saints, op. cit.*, Vol. 2, pp. 478-480.

32. Orson F. Whitney, *Saturday Night Thoughts, a Series of Dissertations on Spiritual, Historical and Philosophic Themes*, Deseret News, Salt Lake City, Utah, 1921, pp. 138-145, 174.

33. Joseph Fielding Smith, *The Way to Perfection, Short Discourses on Gospel Themes*, Genealogical Society of Utah. Salt Lake City, Utah 1949 (8th edition), p. 130. (See also 3rd edition: 1940.)

turned aside from the main body . . . and by and by mingled with the Gentiles and became the leaven to leaven with the promised seed all the nations of the earth."

Is it altogether improbable that in that journey of one and a half years, as Esdras states it, from Media the land of their captivity to the frozen north, some of the backsliding Israel rebelled, turned aside from the main body, forgot their God, by and by mingled with the Gentiles and became the leaven to leaven with the promised seed all the nations of the earth? The account given in the Book of Mormon of a single family of this same house, its waywardness, its stiffneckedness before God, its internal quarrels and family feuds are, we fear, an example on a small scale of what most probably happened in the vast bodies of Israelites who for so many months wended their tedious way northward. Laman and Lemuel had, no doubt, many counterparts in the journeying Ten Tribes. And who so likely to rebel as stubborn, impetuous, proud and warlike Ephraim? Rebellion and backsliding have been so characteristically the story of Ephraim's career that we can scarcely conceive that it could be otherwise and yet preserve the unities of that people's history. Can it be any wonder then that so much of the blood of Ephraim has been found hidden and unknown in the midst of the nations of northern Europe and other parts until the spirit of prophecy revealed its existence? . . .

As abundant proof that many were led by God from the land of promise before the days of the captivity we have the words of Nephi:

"For it appears that the house of Israel, sooner or later, will be scattered upon all the face of the earth, and also among all nations. And behold, there are many who are already lost from the knowledge of those who are at Jerusalem. Yea, the more part of all the tribes have been led away; and they are scattered to and fro upon the isles of the sea; and whither they are none of us knoweth, save that we know that they have been led away. And since they have been led away, these things have been prophesied concerning them, and also concerning all those who shall hereafter be scattered and be confounded." [1 Nephi 22:3-5]

Also the testimony of his brother Jacob:

"And now, my beloved brethren, seeing that our merciful God has given us so great knowledge concerning these things, let us remember him, and lay aside our sins, and not hang down our heads, for we are not cast off; nevertheless, we have been driven out of the land of our inheritance; but we have been led to a better land, for the Lord has made the sea our path, and we are upon an isle of the sea. But great are the promises of the Lord unto them who are upon the isles of the sea; wherefore as it says isles, there must needs be more than this, and they are inhabited also by our brethren. For behold, the Lord God has led away from time to time from the house of Israel, according to his will and pleasure. And now behold, the Lord remembereth all them who have been broken off, wherefore he remembereth us also." [2 Nephi 10:20-22]

That we may better understand the various partial and subsequent general captivities of Israel and Judah. the following short statement thereof is here inserted. The dates given are those of the commonly accepted chronology:

Pul, of Sardanapalus, imposed a tribute on Menahen, king of Israel, about 770 B.C.

Tiglath Pileser carried away the tribes living east of the Jordan and in Galilee, B.C. 740.

Shalmaneser twice invaded the kingdom of Israel, took Samaria, after three years' siege, and carried the people captive to Assyria from the Jewish cities that he captured.

Nebuchadnezzar, in the first half of his reign (B.C. 605-562), repeatedly invaded Judea, besieged Jerusalem and carried its inhabitants to Babylon.[34]

In addition to Elder Reynolds' comments, Elder James E. Talmage, an Apostle, has similarly expressed that although "by worldwide dispersion the children of Israel have been mingled with the nations" of the world, nevertheless, "a sufficient number" of the Lost Ten Tribes "were led away as a body and are now in existence in some place where the Lord has hidden them:"

The Lord has designated the people of Israel as especially His own. With Abraham He entered into a covenant and said: "I will make of thee a great nation, and I will bless thee, and make thy name great; and thou shalt be a blessing: And I will bless them that bless thee, and curse him that curseth thee: and in thee shall all families of the earth be blessed." This was to be an everlasting covenant. It was confirmed upon Isaac, and in turn upon Jacob who was called Israel. The promises regarding the multitudinous posterity, amongst whom were to be counted many of exalted rank, have been literally fulfilled. No less certain is the realization of the second part of the prediction, that in and

---

34. George Reynolds. *op. cit.,* pp. 10-11, 20-21; Bruce R. McConkie, *op. cit.,* p. 457.

through Abraham's descendants should all nations of the earth be blessed. For, by worldwide dispersion the children of Israel have been mingled with the nations; and the blood of the covenant people has been sprinkled among the peoples. And now, in this the day of the gathering, when the Lord is again bringing His people together to honor and bless them above all that the world can give, every nation with the blood of Israel in the veins of its members will partake of the blessings . . .

While many of those belonging to the Ten Tribes were diffused among the nations, a sufficient number to justify the retention of the original name were led away as a body and are now in existence in some place where the Lord has hidden them. To them the resurrected Christ went to minister after His visit to the Nephites, as before stated. Their return constitutes a very important part of the gathering, characteristic of the dispensation of the fullness of times.[35]

In conclusion, probably as Elder George Reynolds has stated, the Israelites of the tribe of Ephraim were "so characteristically... rebellious and backsliding" that some of them "turned aside from the main body" of the Ten Tribes as it traveled northwards.[36] For the writer Baruch, in the Apocrypha, has stated that there were eventually only "nine and a half tribes, which were across the river Ephrates" and who became lost to the rest of mankind. (Baruch 78:1, *Apocrypha*) However, whether there were precisely nine-and-a-half tribes, ten tribes, or more or less than these of the Lost Tribes who traveled northward is debatable, since Latter-day scripture and other Apocrypha writings identify the number of tribes that became lost as being "ten" in number.[37] (D&C 110:11; 2 Esdras 13:40)

---

35. James E. Talmage, *Articles of Faith*, Deseret Book Company. Salt Lake City. Utah, 1961, pp. 339-341. W. Cleon Skousen has likewise written: "Thus the remnants of these apostate Israelites disappeared into the mysterious limbo of the great unknown. It has been thought by many authorities that they completely lost their identity by mixing with other peoples, and it is true that we seem to find fragments of them scattered across the face of the earth. Nevertheless. the Lord has assured us in modern revelation that eventually their location and identity will be revealed and we will find that in spite of the mixing process, the majority have maintained their integrity as a distinct people . . ." (*Fourth Thousand Years, op. cit.,* p. 500.)

36. George Reynolds. *op. cit.,* pp. 10-11.

37. This author has chosen the number "ten" because it is a rounded number and appears in two out of three Apocrypha and scriptural references used in identifying the number of the "lost tribes." (Baruch 78:1; 2 Esdras 13:40: D&C 110:11)

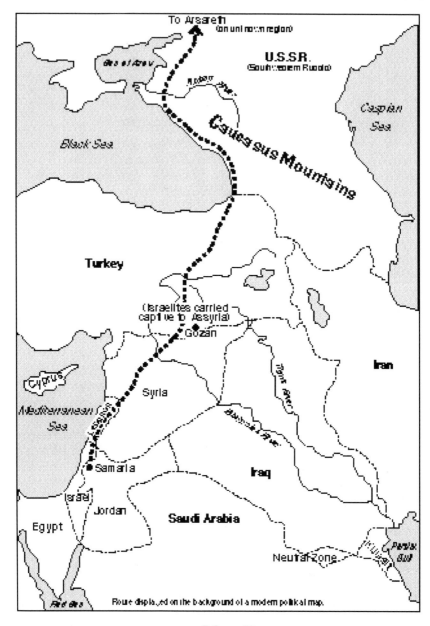

Map B
**The Possible Route of the Ten Tribes of Israel:
Covering Their Journey from Palestine to Arsareth**

Three

Theories:
The Location
Of The Lost Tribes

A Precaution to the Wise

As explained in Chapter Two of this book, the Ten Tribes of Israel escaped from their Assyrian captivity sometime prior to 610 B.C., and with Divine assistance crossed the Euphrates River, and possibly passed around the westward side of the Caucasus Mountain Range in southwestern Russia. Thenafter, the Ten Tribes traveled in a northerly direction through an unknown geographical region called "Arsareth" for approximately a year-and-a-half, wherein at "least a sufficient number or large portion" of the people eventually became "lost" to the rest of mankind.

Today, as in the past, the present geographical location of the Lost Ten Tribes is still a subject of continued debate and speculation among biblical and secular scholars throughout the world. In fact, even though the Lord *has not yet revealed* to His own Church where the Lost Ten Tribes are presently located,[1] this has not deterred a number of General Authorities and members of the Church, since the time of the Prophet Joseph Smith up to our day, from often expressing their own personal beliefs, positions, opinions, theories or speculations as to where the Lost Ten Tribes may be presently located.

Consequently, since this book is concerned with the Lost Ten Tribes and the teachings or statements of the Brethren (in whatever context or form they have appeared relative to this subject), this chapter will discuss what the leaders and members of the Church, as well as others, have said regarding the present *possible* location of the Lost Ten Tribes of Israel.

---

1. D.C. 110:11, 113:10, 36; 1 Nephi 22:4. Bruce R. McConkie, *op cit.*, p. 455. See also Chapter 2, footnote 29 in this book.

However, before proceeding further, the reader may benefit by considering the following statement, which has been given so that the material cited within this particular chapter may be understood in its proper perspective:

The fact that General Authorities of the Church have sometimes discussed subjects as a matter of personal opinion, has occasionally caused some distress among Latter-day Saints, particularly those who have not understood the difference of, or appreciated the fact, that the Brethren of the Church are just as entitled to express their own personal opinions on an unrevealed subject as they are to declare the inspired word of the Lord on a Gospel truth . . . .

It is therefore important to know how to tell the difference . . . .

For example, when the Brethren have spoken or written upon an unrevealed subject of then current speculation, such as . . . the location of the Lost Ten Tribes and the north country . . . that nearly, if not on every occasion when so doing, they have been careful to either pronounce some type of reservation about the topic or contents they would be discussing, by using such cautionary words as: "maybe, likely, could be, possible, etc.," or have come right out and stated that it was their "own opinion or feeling" regarding the subject then in question . . . . Any one of these precautionary measures used by the Brethren are indicative of the fact that they were speaking their own mind, and not necessarily that of the Lord's . . . .

Unfortunately, some well meaning but otherwise misguided members of the Church, when speaking or writing upon unrevealed subjects, have on too many occasions not used even one of these precautionary discretions, but have instead spoken in terminology as if certain things were revealed and were definitely "facts" when "in fact' they were far from being so . . . . These statements and writings have proved to be a disservice to other Latter-day Saints who, not having enough background in the Gospel, have accepted them as being true . . . . It is a dangerous thing to ever state as a fact a personal theory or opinion about a particular subject in which the Lord has not yet revealed the necessary light and knowledge sufficient for truthful and intelligent judgement . . . .[2]

---

2. Quotations from a letter by the author, addressed to Patrick D. Blakely, dated: August 16, 1977, pp. 2-3. A copy of this letter is in the possession of this author.

It is therefore the hope of this author that all those who read this chapter will exercise great caution, wisdom, and a prayerful attitude before deciding to accept any of the beliefs and/or opinions expressed by the various individuals quoted herein. For indeed, the "present location of the Lost Ten Tribes" is in fact an "unrevealed subject of current speculation!"

A Brief Review of Some Early Theories Proposed by Biblical and Secular Historians as to the Location of the Lost Ten Tribes

To place in proper perspective the major theories that have been proposed by Latter-day Saints to explain the present location of the "Lost Ten Tribes" and/or "the north country" (from which the Lost Tribes shall return sometime in these last days), it is first advantageous to briefly review some of the best-known theories proposed earlier by other religious and secular historians. Concerning these earlier theories put forth by individuals who were not Latter-day Saints, Walt Whipple, an L.D.S. author and scholar, has briefly summarized them as follows:

Lost Tribes hunting is not a "modern pastime." Early Baptist missionaries to Burma were sure they had found the Lost Ten Tribes in the Red Karens. G. Moore in 1861 was similarly hasty in his decision that the Afghan stock of India represented the whole of the "lost ten tribes." N. McLeod in 1879 made a like claim for a certain caste among the Japanese. The Abyssinians have been thus classed because of their Judaistic traits. Further south in 1904, the "lost tribes" were to have been discovered among the warrior-Masai by M. Merker . . . .

Joseph Smith was not the first to claim that the American Indians were of Israelitish stock. Father Duran in 1585, Charles Beatty in 1768, James Adair in 1775, Charles Crawford in 1801, Elias Boudinot in 1816, Reverand Ethan Smith in 1825 are but a few who theorized that the Indians were the Lost Ten Tribes. Of course, when the Book of Mormon was published, its believers could readily see that the Lamanites were of Israelitish stock but were not the "lost ten tribes . . . ."

[In another perspective] Asahel Grant in 1841 and Allen H. Godbey in 1930 differed in their tangents but agreed in the main that the "ten tribes" were never lost. Their reasoning is as follows:

A. Nowhere in the Bible is there mention of the ten tribes as being [specifically] "lost."

B. After their conquest of Assyria, the Bible does not mention them moving elsewhere.

C. Paul before King Agrippa stated that the "twelve tribes" were serving God night and day. [Acts 26:7]

D. King Agrippa himself according to Josephus exhorted loyalty to the Romans and discouraged the Jews from hoping for help from their fellow-tribes beyond the Euphrates river, because the Parthian would not permit them to leave.

E. James addressed his Epistle to the "twelve tribes" scattered abroad. [James 1:1]

F. Josephus in the first century claimed to have known their location, he said: ". . . the entire body of the people of Israel remained in that country, wherefore there are but two tribes in Asia and Europe subject to the Romans, while the ten tribes are beyond Euphrates till now, and are an immense multitude, and not to be estimated by numbers . . . ."

G. In the fifth century, Jerome treated the dispersed Jews and the ten Tribes with these words: "Unto this day the ten tribes are subject to the kings of the Persians, nor has their captivity ever been loosed." And again he says, "The ten tribes inhabit at this day the cities and mountains of the Medes."

And Godbey further stated: At no period has Oriental Judaism admitted that any tribes were lost. The egotism of modern western gentile ignorance invented the theory of lost tribes . . . they promptly and unanimously agreed that the ten tribes of Israel never were lost; they remained in the east, and are there yet.

Grant continued even further and quoted many scriptural references speaking of the return of Israel from Assyria and states that the Nestorians are the only inhabitants of Assyria now, and therefore they must be the ten tribes. Another theory similar to the above but for the purpose of disproving British Israelism, was expounded by Reverend F. W. Pitt. He attempted to show that by intermarriage the ten tribes had amalgamated with the "two tribes" (of the Kingdom of Judah) and in that way had lost their name and distinction.[3]

---

3. Walt Whipple, *A Discussion of the Many Theories Concerning the Whereabouts of the Lost Ten Tribes.* (A Research Paper completed at Brigham Young University, 1958-1959.) B.Y.U. Library Reference Number: Mormon. M238.4, W57L., (35 pages total.), pp. 1-3. (Whipple received his B.A. and M.A. degrees in 1958 and 1959, in Church History and Doctrine.

The Major Theories Proposed by Latter-day Saints

When The Church of Jesus Christ of Latter-day Saints was first organized in 1830, a number of its prospective members had already heard of some of the various gentile (non-Latter-day Saint) theories that had been proposed to explain the whereabouts of the Lost Ten Tribes.[4] However, with the first edition of the Book of Mormon published in 1830, it was not very long until new members of the Church learned that the previous theories of gentile authors, for the most part, were incorrect. The Book of Mormon revealed, to its believers and skeptics alike, that (1) the Ten Tribes had been led away by the Lord and were in fact "lost" to mankind (1 Nephi 22:3; 3 Nephi 15:15,17:4); (2) that following His resurrection the Lord had personally visited the Lost Ten Tribes (3 Nephi 17:4; 15:15); (3) that they were and are maintaining scriptural records of their own (2 Nephi 29:13); and (4) that the Gospel is continually being preached to them preparatory to their return in the last days (3 Nephi 21:26-28).

A few years later, the Prophet Joseph Smith received by revelation Doctrine & Covenants sections 133 (in 1831) and 110 (in 1836), and Latter-day Saints additionally learned that the Lost Tribes still consisted of approximately "ten" Tribes (D&C 110:11), and that their return to "Zion" (the American continent) from the "north country" in the Last Days would be preceded by astonishing and miraculous events (D&C 133:26-34; 110:11).

This new scriptural information dispelled many incorrect beliefs previously held by a number of Latter-day Saints, and served to strengthen their testimonies as to the circumstances and present actuality of the Lost Ten Tribes. However, it did not put a stop to the speculation by members of the Church as to where the Lost Ten Tribes, or even the "north country," were specifically located.

Thus, as can be expected, many members and General Authorities then and up to our present day have continued to express their own personal theories, beliefs, opinions, etc., as to the precise whereabouts of the Lost Ten Tribes. The best known and most prevalent of these theories formally and currently advanced by Latter-day Saints in Mormon literature, may be categorized under the following four general headings:

---

4. Walt Whipple, *Ibid.,* p. 3.

1. **The Unknown Planet Theory**—(sometimes incorrectly called the *"North Star Theory"*), which proposes that the Lost Ten Tribes were taken away from this earth in a manner similar to that of the City of Enoch, and that they now reside on another planet, orb, sphere, and or near another star somewhere in the universe.

2. **The Hollow Earth (or Concave) Theory**—which proposes that the Lost Ten Tribes possibly reside in either an unknown concave area, like in a volcano, or in a great hollow area, somewhere in the region of the North Pole.

3. **The North Pole Theory**—which proposes that the Lost Ten Tribes possibly live in a mysteriously-camouflaged area somewhere near or at the North Pole.

4. **The Dispersion Theory**—which proposes that the Lost Ten Tribes are today totally scattered among the present nations of the earth, and are only lost as to their identity—not as to their location—and are presently being gathered into the Church through missionary labors.[5]

This author will now attempt to review these above four theories in a rather comprehensive and detailed manner. However, please remember that the theories, beliefs, opinions, etc., expressed in this chapter by various General Authorities and others of the Church are their own personal opinions and or views, and are not necessarily the product of divine revelation. In addition, it should be recognized by all that some of the statements attributed to the Prophet Joseph Smith and other Brethren of the Church, as recorded by other individuals, are of a secondary (hearsay) nature, that they at times evince internal illogic, and sometimes conflict with prior statements attributed to the same individual, thereby making some if

5. Walt Whipple. *Ibid.*, pp. 1-5. R. Clayton Brough, "The Results of a Survey of Latter-day Saint Opinion on the Present Possible Whereabouts of the Lost Ten Tribes of Israel." An independent monograph written by the author, dated: July 14, 1978, total 9 pages. Summaries and conclusions relative to the various theories described were obtained first through oral interviews and then by a cross-sectional survey of Latter-day Saints twenty-one years of age and older living in various Wards in Utah, Idaho and California, from January 1978 to June 1978. An example of one of the survey sheets is contained in this book under the section entitled *Appendix*. Brief numerical results of the survey: Results showed that of more than two-hundred Latter-day Saints who responded to having a "specific opinion or belief regarding the present possible location of the Lost Ten Tribes," 53% agreed with the *Dispersion Theory;* 29% agreed with the *Unknown Planet Theory;* 11% agreed with the *North Pole Theory;* 4% agreed with the *Hollow Earth Theory;* and 2% had *another opinion* (which was more or less a sub-theory or combination of one or more of the preceding theories). 58% of those responding were between the ages of 21 to 40; 42% were 41 years of age or older.

not many of these "attributed" statements spurious and question-able as to their authenticity or believeability. Indeed, when judging the truthfulness of these "attributed" statements, one should be careful to "let the spirit beareth record of the truth of those things said and written." (See D&C 9:8-9; 1:39; 59:24; 18:2)

The Unknown Planet Theory

Latter-day Saint proponents of the so-called "unknown Planet Theory" generally believe that the Lost Ten Tribes were taken away from this earth in a manner similar to that of the City of Enoch (which, according to Elder Orson Pratt, an Apostle, and other General Authorities, "was translated or taken away from the earth . . ." and is now "held in reserve, in some part or portion of space . . . not yet revealed;")[6] and that the Lost Tribes now reside on another planet, orb, sphere, and/or near another star somewhere in the universe.[7] (This theory is sometimes referred to as the *North Star Theory*, which is somewhat of a misnomer.)

Proponents of the Unknown Planet Theory, which appears today to be the second most believed of the four major theories advanced to explain the present whereabouts of the Lost Ten Tribes,[8] offer the following evidence in behalf of its support.

---

6. Regarding the City of Enoch and its being "taken away from the earth," Elder Orson Pratt has stated: "How much of the earth was taken up in connec-tion with [the City of Enoch] . . . we are not informed. It might have been a large region. You may ask—'Where was this city of Zion built in ancient days?' According to new revelation it was built upon this great western hemisphere. When I speak of this western hemisphere I speak of it as it now exists. In those days the land was united; the eastern and the western hemisphere were one; but they dwelt in that portion of our globe that is now called the western hemisphere, and they were taken up from this portion of the globe. No doubt all the region of country occupied by them was translated, or taken away from the earth. Does this prove that they were immortal beings from the time of their translation? No; it does not prove any such things. How are we to know anything about it? We can not learn anything in relation to it, except by revelation. God has revealed to us that they are held in reserve, in some part or portion of space; their location is not revealed, but they are held in reserve to be revealed in the latter times, to return to their ancient mother earth; all the inhabitants that were then taken away are to return to the earth." (Orson Pratt, *Journal of Discourses*, July 19, 1874, Vol. 17:147.) And Elder Parley P. Pratt similarly stated: "These [portions of the earth] all must be restored again at the times of the restitution of all things. This will restore the ten tribes of Israel; and also bring again Zion, even Enoch's city. It will bring back the Tree of Life . . . that you and I may partake of it." (*Millennial Star*, Vol. 1, Number 1, p. 258.)

7. Walt Whipple, *op. cit.*, p. 5. R. Clayton Brough, "The Results of a Survey . . . ," *op. cit.*

8. *Ibid.* Of these L.D.S. surveyed, 29% agreed with the Unknown Planet Theory; see footnote #5, on p. 42.

The belief that the Lost Ten Tribes were taken by the Lord from this earth and placed somewhere else in the universe, apparently had its beginning in the early days of the Church. For example, by the early 1850's, Eliza R. Snow, a wife of the Prophet Joseph Smith, had written a poetic song which stated that "when the Lord saw fit to hide the Ten Lost Tribes away" He did so in a manner similar to His removal of the City of Enoch, by "severing" the earth "to provide an orb on which they (the Lost Ten Tribes now) stay." Her song was first published in 1856, as Hymn number 313, in the old music-less Church hymnbook entitled *L.D.S. Hymns: Sacred Hymns and Spiritual Songs of The Church of Jesus Christ of Latter-day Saints.* The following is a quotation of the first part of Sister Snow's song, which was published in succeeding editions of L.D.S. Hymns until 1912, when the Hymn book was then considerably shortened and musical scores were added to the retained songs.

HYMN 313 (C.M.)
First Part.

1. Thou, Earth, wast once a glorious sphere
   Of noble magnitude,
   And didst with majesty appear
   Among the worlds of God.

2. But thy dimensions have been torn
   Asunder, piece by piece,
   And each dismember'd fragment borne
   Abroad to distant space.

3. When Enoch could no longer stay
   Amid corruption here,
   Part of thyself was borne away
   To form another sphere.

4. That portion where his city stood
   He gain'd by right approv'd;
   And nearer to the throne of God
   His planet upward mov'd.

5. And when the Lord saw fit to hide
    The "ten lost tribes" away,
    Thou, Earth, wast sever'd to provide
    The orb on which they stay.

6. And thus, from time to time, thy size
    Has been diminish'd, till
    Thou seemst the law of sacrifice
    Created to fulfill.[9]

It is a fact that the above song by Eliza R. Snow eventually attracted the attention and acknowledgment of many Latter-day Saints. For example, in 1909, Elder Matthias F. Cowley, an Apostle, had published the book: *Wilford Woodruff, History of His Life and Labors*. While preparing this book on the life of the former Church President, Elder Cowley found that the latter had recorded in one of his journals a comment which had once been made by President Brigham Young in Logan, Utah. It was in regards to this statement by President Young that President Woodruff wrote the following words in his journal:

The leaders upon their return from Provo made a visit to Logan. Here, President Young is quoted as saying that the ten tribes of Israel are on a portion of the earth—a portion separated from the main land. This view is also expressed in one of the sacramental hymns written by Eliza R. Snow:

And when the Lord saw fit to hide
The ten lost tribes away,
Thou, earth, was severed to provide
The orb on which they stay.[10]

This view that the Lost Ten Tribes are separated from the earth upon which we now reside has also been attributed to the Prophet Joseph Smith. One of the supports indicated for this thesis is that since Eliza R. Snow was one of the wives of the Prophet Joseph Smith, where better could she have learned this belief that the Lost

---

9. Franklin D. Richards, L D.S. Hymns: *Sacred hymns & Spiritual Songs for The Church of Jesus Christ of Latter-day Saints*. Liverpool England, (later by Deseret News Company of S L C., Utah.), 1856, Eleventh Edition, Hymn #313 (CM), p. 386. (This same hymn appeared in succeeding years as Hymn #322, then Hymn #323 up until 1912.)

10. Matthias F. Cowley, *Wilford Woodruff*, Bookcraft, Salt Lake City, Utah, 196, p. 448.

Ten Tribes were "sever'd" from this earth and placed on another "orb on which they [now] stay" than from her own husband?"[11] Proponents of this view also state that not only did the Prophet teach this belief to his wives, but that he also taught this to a number of his closest friends within the Church. The following two statements have been offered as evidence in support of this viewpoint:

[This first statement is attributed to Homer M. Brown, a Patriarch of Granite Stake and grandson of Mr. and Mrs. Benjamin Brown, who once gave refuge to the Prophet Joseph Smith:]

Brother Brown, will you give us some light and explanation of the 5th verse on page 386 of the Hymn Book which formed another planet, [sic] according to the Hymn of Eliza R. Snow.

Yes. sir, I think I can answer your question. Sister Eliza R. Snow, in visiting my grandparents, was asked by my grandmother: "Eliza, where did you get your ideas about the Ten Lost Tribes being taken away as you explain it in your wonderful hymn?"

She answered as follows: "Why, my husband (The Prophet Joseph) told me about it."

Have you any other information that your grandfather ever gave you, as contained in any conversation with the Prophet Joseph Smith?

"I have! One evening in Nauvoo, just after dark, somebody rapped at the door very rigorously. Grandfather said he was reading the Doctrine and Covenants. He rose hurriedly and answered the summons at the door, where we met the Prophet Joseph Smith."

He said, "Brother Brown, can you keep me over night, the mobs are after me?" Grandfather answered, "Yes sir. It will not be the first time, come in."

"All right," the Prophet said, shutting the door quickly. He came in and sat down. Grandmother said: "Brother Joseph, have you had your supper?"

"No" he answered, "I have not." So she prepared him a meal and he ate it. Afterward they were in conversation relative to the principles of the Gospel. During the conversation the ten lost tribes were mentioned. Grandfather said, "Joseph, where are the ten tribes?" He said, "Come to the door and I will show you, come on Sister Brown, I want you both to see."

11. Leon M. Strong. *Three Timely Treasures,* Zion's Printing & Publishing Company, Independence, Missouri, 1949, p. 30 (See Footnote.) R Clayton Brough, "The Results of a Survey . . .," *op. cit.,* pp. 1-9.

It being a starlight night the Prophet said: "Brother Brown, can you show me the Polar Star?" "Yes sir," he said, pointing to the North Star. "There it is." "Yes, I know" said the Prophet, "But which one? There are a lot of stars there."

Grandfather said: "Can you see the points of the Dipper?" The Prophet answered, "Yes." "Well" he said, "trace the pointers," pointing up to the largest star. "That is the North Star."

The Prophet answered: "You are correct. Now," he said, pointing toward the star, "do you discern a little twinkler to the right and below the Polar Star, which we would judge to be about the distance of 20 feet from here?"

Grandfather answered, "Yes, sir."

The Prophet said: "Sister Brown, do you see that star also?" Her answer was, "Yes, sir."

"Very well then, he said. "let's go in." After re-entering the house, the Prophet said: "Brother Brown, I noticed when I came in that you were reading the Doctrine and Covenants. Will you kindly get it."

He did so. The Prophet turned to Section 133 and read, commencing at the 26th verse, and throughout the 34th verse. He said, after reading the 31st verse, "Now let me ask you what would cause the Everlasting Hills to tremble with more violence than the coming together of the two planets. And the place whereon they reside will return to this Earth." "Now" he said, "Scientists will tell you that it is not scientific: that two planets coming together would be disastrous to both;[12] but, when two planets or other objects are traveling in the same direction and one of them with a little greater velocity than the other, it would

---

12. True. This view is not acceptable to modern science because it defies some of the basic laws or theories of physics and astronomy. For example, "Roche's limit" states, in essence, that if a moon (or smaller satellite) gets too close to its planet (which is larger), it will be broken up by tidal forces and will form a ring around the planet. In other words, if the moon were much closer to Earth, its internal gravity would no longer be able to hold it together. The "back end" would go into an orbit of its own, separate from the middle or the front. The result would be a ring of debris, with each rock in a separate. individually balanced, orbit. The largest pieces left would be those for which the strength of the rock was just able to keep the tidal forces from ripping it apart. Specifically, Roche's limit is the distance of 2.44 times a planet's radius, measured from the planet's center, within which any satellite or heavenly body would be in danger of disruption due to the gravitational force of the planet. Currently there is no known case of a satellite existing within the Roche limit of a planet, though Saturn's rings lie well inside, and may be the debris of a former satellite which was pulled to pieces.

not be disastrous, because the one traveling faster would over-take the other. Now, what would cause the mountains of ice to melt quicker than the heat caused by the friction of the two planets coming together?" And then he asked the question: "Did you ever see a meteor falling that was not red hot? So that would cause the mountains of ice to melt."

"And relative to the Great Highway which should be cast up when the planet returns to its place in the great Northern Waters, it will form a highway and waters will recede and roll back." He continued, "Now as to their coming back from the Northern Waters; they will return from the north because their planet will return to the place from whence it was taken."

Relative to the waters rolling back to the north. If you take a vessel of water and swing it rapidly around your head you won't spill any, but if you stop the motion gradually, it will begin to pour out. "Now," he said, "Brother Brown, at the present time this earth is rotating very rapidly. When this planet returns it will make the earth that much heavier, and it will then revolve slower, and that will account for the waters receding from the earth for a great while . . . ." [13]

And Elder Orson Pratt, as an Apostle, once wrote that:

The Prophet Joseph [Smith] once in my hearing advanced his opinion that the Ten Tribes were separated from the Earth; or a portion of the Earth was by a miracle broken off, and that the Ten Tribes were taken away with it, and that in the latter days it would be restored to the Earth or be let down in the Polar regions. Whether the Prophet founded his opinion upon revelation or whether it was a matter of mere speculation with him, I am not able to say. [14]

---

13. Robert W. Smith. *Scriptural and Secular Prophecies Pertaining to The Last Days,* Pyramid Press, Salt Lake City, Utah. 1948 (10th edition), pp. 211-216. Walt Whipple. op. cit., pp. 6-7. R. Clayton Brough, "The Results of a Survey . . . ," *op. cit. Note:* As can be seen from this statement (even if we believed in its validity), the Prophet Joseph Smith, as supposedly quoted, never stated or even inferred that the Lost Ten Tribes were located "on" or in" the North (Polar) Star" or any "star" for that matter. Instead, he discusses the view of "two planets' coming together," and that the ten tribes were on a portion of this earth, that had been taken away, and that someday will return. Hence the somewhat misnomer for the title of this view: "The North Star Theory."

14. Orson Pratt, *Letter Box of Orson Pratt,* Church Historian's Office, Letter to John C. Hall, December 13. 1875. (Information presented to this author by Vern Swanson.)

There are three other statements in Mormon literature by General Authorities, which discuss this possibility that the Lost Ten Tribes are presently located on some other sphere than this earth. The earliest of these statements was by Elder Parley P. Pratt, an Apostle, who, as editor of the *Millennial Star* in 1841, was asked by Joseph Fielding how the "stars" could "fall from heaven to earth, when they are much larger than the earth?" Elder Pratt answered his question with the following editorial:

> We are nowhere given to understand that all the stars will fall or even many of them: but only "as a fig tree casteth her UNTIMELY figs when she is shaken with a mighty wind." The stars which will fall to the earth, are fragments, which have been broken off from the earth from time to time, in the mighty convulsions of nature. Some in the days of Enoch, some perhaps in the days of Peleg, some with the ten tribes, and some at the crucifixion of the Messiah. These all must be restored again at the "times of restitution of ALL THINGS." This will restore the ten tribes of Israel; and also bring again Zion, even Enoch's city. It will bring back the tree of life which is in the midst of the paradise of God; that you and I may partake of it. [See Rev. II, 7.] When these fragments, (some of which are vastly larger than the present earth) are brought back and joined to this earth, it will cause a convulsion of all nature; the graves of the Saints will be opened, and they rise from the dead; while the mountains will flow down, the valleys rise, the sea retire to its own place, the islands and continents will be removed, and earth be rolled together as a scroll. The earth will be many times larger than it is now.—"If I have told you of earthly things and ye believe not; what would you think if you were to be told of heavenly things?"[15]

In addition to Elder Pratt's statement, President Wilford Woodruff wrote in 1859 that "A portion of the North Country containing the ten tribes may be separated from the Earth;" while Elder Brigham H. Roberts wrote in 1912, that " . . . there are those I believe, who . . . have held that perhaps the ten lost tribes were located upon some detached portion of the earth. As to that, l have no opinion to express.[16]

---

15. Pariey P. Pratt, *Millennial Star*, Vol. 1, p. 258, February, 1841.

16. Wilford Woodruff, *His Daily Journal*, September 25, 1859. (Church Historian's Office. (Information presented to this author by Vern Swanson.) Brigham H. Roberts, *Defense of the Faith and the Saints, op. cit*, Vol. 2, pp. 447-480.

The Narrow Neck Proposition, A Sub-Theory

Associated with the Unknown Planet Theory, but somewhat removed from its basic premise that the Lost Ten Tribes are now supposedly on a "portion of the earth" that has been "separate, detached or taken away from our globe," and placed on some other "planet, orb, sphere, and/or near another star somewhere in the universe," is the "Narrow Neck Proposition."[17] This "proposition" (perhaps better referred to as a kind of "sub-theory" of the main Unknown Planet Theory) states that "attached" to the earth by a narrow neck of land" are two spheres (invisible or otherwise) which vary in size—one which is connected to the earth "north of the north pole," and the other which is connected to our globe "south of the south pole."[18]

This proposition is based on a drawing which the Prophet Joseph Smith supposedly drew about the year 1842, and which was later secured and preserved by Philo Dibble, of Springville, Utah. Dibble later made a copy of the drawing in 1884 which he then gave to Matthew W. Dalton, a resident of Willard, Utah, who eventually published it in 1906. Dalton states that Dibble informed him the Prophet said that in the drawing [see Figure A], the sphere marked "A" represented the earth, and that the Ten Tribes were on the sphere marked "B." He did not state the purpose for sphere "C," but others have thought it to be the location of the City of Enoch.[19] The following is the history and meaning of the drawing as given by Matthew Dalton, with appropriate affidavits added:

[By Matthew Dalton:]

Now, how was the diagram obtained? The Prophet Joseph Smith drew the original drawing a short time before his death, or in 1842, in the presence of several witnesses, Philo Dibble, of Springville, Utah, was one of these witnesses. and secured the drawing. In the month of May, of the year 1884, he made a copy thereof for me, the diagram herein shown being the result, with the possible exception that the spheres marked B and C were perhaps somewhat smaller than shown herein. At the time the original drawing was made the brethren were discussing the dis-

---

17. R Clayton Brough, "The Results of a Survey . . . ," *op cit.*

18. Matthew W. Dalton, *The Period of God s Work on This Planet (or How Science Agrees With The Revelations of Our Beloved Redeemer) A Key to This Earth.* Utah, 1906, pp. 11-12, 86-88.

19. *Ibid.* Walt Whipple. *op. cit.*, pp. 8-9.

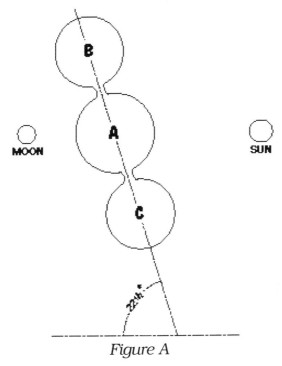

Figure A

appearance of the Ten Tribes and wondering where they were, upon which the Prophet made the drawing and stated that the Ten Tribes were located on the sphere marked B.

Some may, and even do, doubt the truth of the diagram of the spheres A and B and C, and even the statement as to how the diagram was obtained. Yet it is nevertheless true. It was drawn in the presence of William and Sarah Beecher and myself in the year 1884 by Philo Dibble, above shown as a resident of Springville, Utah County, Utah. His son, Sidney Dibble, who is now alive and a resident of Springville, went before a notary public and on oath testified that this diagram of A, B and C, was a true facsimile of a drawing made by his father.[20]

AFFIDAVITS
UNITED STATES OF AMERICA

STATE OF UTAH,
COUNTY OF UTAH, } **SS**

---

20. Matthew W. Dalton, *op. cit.*, pp. 11-12, 86-88.

Sidney Dibble, of Springville, Utah County, State of Utah, after being first duly sworn, on oath says, that M. W. Dalton, of Willard, Utah, has shown him a drawing drawn by C. F. Wells, Jr., of Willard, Utah, representing to be a drawing of the earth and a sphere north of the north pole, and a sphere south of the south pole, both spheres connected to the earth by a narrow neck of land, and I hereby certify that the drawing shown me by M. W. Dalton is a facsimile of a drawing shown me by my father Philo Dibble. which he told me was given him by the Prophet Joseph Smith about the year A.D. 1842, with the exception that both the northern spheres marked B is a little too large in proportion to the earth; also that the southern sphere, marked C, is also too large in proportion to the earth.

SIDNEY DIBBLE.

Subscribed and sworn to before me, this, 30th day of January, A.D.1906.

JAMES CAFFREY,
NOTARY PUBLIC

STATE OF UTAH
COUNTY OF WEBER. }   **SS**

I, M. W. Dalton, of Willard, Box Elder County, State of Utah, being first duly sworn under oath, depose and say: That I was personally acquainted with Philo Dibble, who was a resident of Springville, Utah County, Utah; that in May,1884, the said Philo Dibble was present at the residence of William Beecher and Sarah Beecher, at Willard, Box Elder County, State of Utah, and there and then, and in their presence, and in my presence, he, the said Philo Dibble, gave and delivered to me an exact, true and correct counterpart of the original drawing of which he, the said Philo Dibble, received from the hand of Joseph Smith, the Prophet, in the year 1842, in the office of the said Joseph Smith, the Prophet, at Nauvoo, Illinois, in the presence of six other prominent Latter-Day Saints.

I, M. W. Dalton, deponent herein, hereby solemnly declare that the drawing in my possession, and which was drawn and marked as drawn by C. F. Wells, Jr., Willard, Utah, is a true, faithful and correct counterpart of the said diagram shown and given me at Willard, Box Elder County, State of Utah, by the said Philo Dibble, a resident of Springville, Utah, at the home of

William Beecher and Sarah Beecher, in their presence, and in my presence, in the month of May, in the year 1884.
This I solemnly swear.

M. W. DALTON.

Subscribed and sworn to before me, this 8th day of March, A.D. 1906.

JOSEPH CHEZ,
NOTARY PUBLIC

My Notarial Commission expires Sept. 24th, 1906.

Some proponents of the "Narrow Neck Proposition" have tried to correlate the previous drawing published by Dalton with the earlier statements attributed to the Prophet Joseph Smith, which fit much better under the basic premise of the Unknown Planet Theory. These proponents speculate that perhaps the narrow neck of land," as shown in the drawing, is a kind of spiritual connection between the two physical spheres (Figure A, marked "B" & "C") and the earth (marked "A"), thus allowing their "proposition" to come into harmony with the basic premise of the Unknown Planet Theory that "the Lost Ten Tribes are on some sphere *physically separated* from this earth."[21]

Suffice it to say, these individuals who propose this view or any of its relative types are indeed only "speculating;" for the recorded gospel sermons and discourses of the Prophet Joseph Smith as well as the four standard (scriptural) works of the Church are silent regarding any of the premises of the Unknown Planet Theory or the Narrow Neck Proposition.[22]

The Hollow Earth (or Concave) Theory

The second theory which has been proposed by various Latter-day Saints to explain the present whereabouts of the Lost Ten Tribes is the so-called "Hollow Earth" or "Concave Earth Theory." This theory proposes that the Lost Ten Tribes either live in a great hollow area somewhere in the region of the North Pole or in an unknown concave area, like a volcano, near or in the North Pole.

The first recorded appearance of this theory which this author could find in Mormon literature was in a related statement contained within a sermon given by Elder Orson Pratt, an Apostle, at

---

21. R. Clayton Brough, "The Results of A Survey. . ." *op. cit.*

22. Extensive review of the scriptures and various works containing the discourses of the Prophet Joseph Smith.

the "New Tabernacle" in Salt Lake City in 1875. In this statement,
Elder Pratt gave it as his opinion that "based upon the information he had received from those [people] who have tried to find a
passage to the [north] pole," that it was possible for the Lord God
to cause deep and extensive valleys, very deep in comparison with
high ranges of mountains around them, where the temperature
would be comparatively mild, the same as in these mountains
here [in Utah]," which would therefore be "fit for habitation" by
such peoples as the Lost Ten Tribes of Israel. Elder Pratt's statement is as follows:

> . . . one thing I do know, from that which is reported by
> those who have tried to find a passage to the pole, that there is
> a warmer country off there, and that birds of passage go north
> to find a warmer climate. That I know from the writings of intel-
> ligent men who have been on voyages of discovery. And I know,
> furthermore, that they have crossed by means of dogs and sleds
> a certain portion of this great band of ice and have come to an
> open sea, which proves that there is a warmer country further
> north. There is a tract of country around the pole, some seven
> or eight hundred miles in diameter, that no man among the
> nations that we are acquainted with, has ever explored. But how
> much of that land may be fit for habitation I am not prepared to
> say, for I do not know. I know it would be a very easy matter for
> the Lord God, by the aid of great mountain ranges encircling
> them around about, to produce a band of ice which would pre-
> vent other nations and people very easily reaching them. I also
> know that it would be a very easy matter for the Lord God to
> cause deep and extensive valleys, very deep in comparison with
> high ranges of mountains around them, where the temperature
> would be comparatively mild, the same as in these mountains
> here. We see all the rigors of an arctic winter on our eastern
> ranges of mountains, while at the same time here are deep val-
> leys in which there is a comparatively warm climate, which
> makes me think of that which was spoken by the mouth of
> Isaiah the Prophet in referring to the latter-day work. He says
> that "when it shall hail, coming down upon the forests, the city
> shall be low in a low place," where the climate is warm.[23]

Following Elder Pratt's statement in 1875, and at least throughout the next two decades, there were apparently a number of some-

23. Orson Pratt, *Journal of Discourses*, Vol.18, p. 26, April 11, 1875.

what similar viewpoints offered by various Latter-day Saints which in one way or another fit into the main category of the "Hollow Earth" (or Concave) Theory."[24] The view that the Lost Ten Tribes possibly existed in a "deep . . . valley" of some type within the region of the north pole, as expressed by Orson Pratt, soon led to or was accompanied by the opinion "that the hole was so deep" that the earth was actually "hollow" somewhere near or at the North Pole.[25]

Among Latter-day Saints, this "Hollow Earth" theory seems to have hit its high peak of propagation or believeability sometime between 1890 and 1910.[26] An example of this is that in 1896 the Church newspaper, the *Deseret Weekly*, published an article written by an unnamed member of the Church (who's initials were W.J.R.) who refuted the then-held belief by "some" members of the Church that the Lost Ten Tribes were "inside" a "hollow" portion of the earth located somewhere "at the northern end" of our globe. The article read:

> Some think the earth hollow and that at the northern end of the earth there is a great hole. They fancy that the earth is inhabited inside with a race of people, said by some to be what is called the ten tribes, as the statement is made that they journeyed to the north for many days and it seems impossible to many to account for them on the land that they now live on.
>
> . . . And if this be so it is more than likely that they are a numberless people. If they are inside the earth, I think that their cry for a long time has been: give us room that we may dwell. I cannot believe that they are in any such a locality . . . . [In adding this theory, the writer of this Era article goes on to state the possibilities of a warmer region in the north. And that some day, explorers may find the Lost Ten Tribes who likewise may also be searching for their brethren of the other two tribes.] [27]

Also during this time, from about 1890 to 1910, some Latter-day Saints called the Hollow Earth Theory the "Symmes Hole

---

24. R. Clayton Brough, "The Hollow Earth Theory," Brigham Young University, Provo, Utah, February, 1975. An independent research paper, with compiled notes regarding the "Hollow Earth Theory," of which a copy is in possession of this author. (6 total pages.)

25. *Ibid.*

26. "The North Pole," *The Deseret Weekly,* Vol. 53, pp. 20-21: June 20, 1896. James H. Anderson, *God's Covenant Race,* Deseret News Press, Salt Lake City, Utah. 1938, p. 115.

27. "The North Pole," *The Deseret Weekly,* Vol. 53, pp. 20-21, June 20, 1896.

Theory,"[28] which theory was named for John C. Symmes, who in 1818 advanced the idea that the earth was "hollow and habitable within, containing a number of solid concentric spheres, one within the other," and that it was "open at the poles 12 or 16 degrees." Today, this idea or theory of Symmes still has "several hundred believers from around . . . the world," who, according to a 1978 newspaper article, are members of a "Hollow Earth Society." The newspaper article reads as follows:

HAMILTON, Ohio (NEA)—When John Cleves Symmes was buried here a century and a half ago, his survivors erected an odd but apt marker on his grave. It's a structure of freestone, surmounted by a metal orb, open at the poles, and dedicated to Symmes' extraordinary theory that the earth is hollow.

A hollow earth? Today the idea is amusing, but in an Amercia [sic] of the early 19th century, when education was scant, when almost any thought was an original thought, John Symmes' absurd proposition was boldly imaginative, and as such enjoyed a popularity not only in the United States but throughout the world.

Oh, people laughed then too. Newspaper editorials of the day called Symmes' theory a "silly dream of a deranged imagination." But when Symmes spoke of "a warm and rich land under our feet," inhabited by "vegetables and animals," he said in essence that we are not alone and thousands chose to believe him.

Never mind that the theory rejected such mathematics as Newton's laws. After all, John Symmes was neither halfwit nor zealot, and in fact was from one of the nation's best families. Symmes' uncle, of the same name, was a Revolutionary War hero, U.S. congressman, and instigator of Ohio's fabled Miami Purchase.

Symmes himself was "high minded, honorable and honest," if the preface of his son's biography is accurate. He was the father of 10 children, a captain during the war of 1812—but he had this passion, his biographer says, this fixed belief that so great an object as earth could not just be a rock throughout.

In 1818, retiring from the military, Symmes composed a letter. "To all the world," he wrote, "I declare the earth is hollow and habitable within, containing a number of solid concentric spheres, one within the other, and that it is open at the poles 12 or 16 degrees." He added: "I pledge my life in support of this theory."

---

28. James H. Anderson, *op. cit.*, p. 115.

Intellectuals hooted, of course, But the idea was not without some historic credentials. The famed English astronomer Edmund Halley (Halley's Comet) believed in the likelihood of a hollow earth. And the great Swiss mathematician Leonhard Euler thought the inner globe was luminous, to give off heat and light.

It's not known whether Symmes copied from the notes of Halley and Euler. At any rate, he believed evidence of the hollow earth was all around. Nature is a conservationist, he said, witness the hollow reeds she makes, the hollow bones and hair. Symmes insisted that a wise Providence does not create perpetual waste.

He told doubters to look to the skies. Saturn has its concentric rings. Mars has what appear to be concentric circles at its poles. And what about Venus? Symmes argued that when Venus is in crescent, its horns are not sharp, but decidedly clipped, probably because of the polar holes to its interior.

Symmes seldom dwelled on the theory of gravity. He believed space was filled with elastic "aether" which held orbicular bodies in place. In the beginning, he said, all matter rotating in this aether formed into concentric spheres. Centrifugal force threw the rotating matter from its axis into hollow balls.

In the case of earth, Symmes said the rotating birth created five hollow spheres, one within another, like Chinese ivory carvings. He said the outer sphere was 1,000 miles thick, and had polar doorways to the inside which were thousands of miles in diameter. Beyond the Arctic, then, he thought there was a shaft through the planet.

Furthermore, the interior spheres were not just empty shells. Symmes pointed out that some Arctic animals migrate north rather than south. Why? Because north is the route to the warm inside. *Symmes' son, the biographer, believed the lost tribes of Israel, who "went up the Euphrates to the north," lived in one of the hollows.* [Italics added]

Symmes labored with his theory for 11 years. He petitioned Congress to fund exploration of the poles, in the name of public interest, but though his argument was soberly introduced, the matter was tabled. Symmes' petitions were also turned down by the General Assembly of Ohio, and by the government of Russia.

Apparently, two members of John Quincy Adams' cabinet were ready to finance a national ship of exploration. But when Andrew Jackson became president, the idea was scotched.

Symmes continued to lecture through the nation, at 50 cents a head, but hope was gone. He died at age 49, still convinced, but unfulfilled.

And yet the hollow earth theory did not die with him. People as disparate as Adolf Hitler and today's UFO logists have since argued the postulation. In 1967 an obscure magazine published a report of an underground city near Portland, Ore., which was inhabited by one million subterranean people.

There is even a Hollow Earth Society now. It claims a membership of several hundred believers from around, if not from inside, the world. Symmes was right, members say. He was ridiculed and scorned, but, well, so was Galileo, and, for that matter, Newton. "Symzonia," they insist, is still down there waiting to be found.[29]

JOHN SYMMES' GRAVE is topped by a fitting marker. A captain during the war of 1812, he devoted his life to supporting the theory that the earth is hollow. The idea was popular enough at the time to interest two members of John Quincy Adams' cabinet in financing a polar expedition. Andrew Jackson scotched the idea.

---

29. Tom Tiede, "John Symmes Proposition That The Earth Is Hollow Still Has Its Supporters." Newspaper Enterprise Association. July 10, 1978.

By the mid-1920s the "hollow earth theory" had been accompanied, if not superceded, by a similar theory which was proposed by both Latter-day Saints and non-Mormons alike, which stated that there was possibly an area in the north pole wherein "volcano heat provides the necessary warmth for an unknown people, who live in a volcano-surrounded center of hidden land." [30] This theory was mentioned in an article which appeared in the *Improvement Era* magazine of the Church in January 1924. In the *Era* article entitled "Are There a People in the Far North?" the editor of the Era, Edward H. Anderson, discussed the "Lost Ten Tribes of Israel and the Far North," and in the course of his discussion reviewed an article which had appeared earlier in the *Popular Science Monthly* magazine dated December, 1923. The *Popular Science Monthly* article told of a theory circulating in those days among the general public and scientific communities of the United States and elsewhere, that there were possibly people living in the region of the north pole on land which was heated by volcanic heat. Of this theory which was presented in the *Popular Science Monthly*, editor Anderson wrote the following:

A theory that volcano heat provides the necessary warmth for an unknown people, who live in a volcano-surrounded center of this hidden land, is advanced. Fifty thousand square miles, or about the size of the state of Pennsylvania, is said to be a rough estimate of the size of the land—an undulating, fertile plateau, steam-heated by hot springs, geysers and boiling pools, and rimmed by a volcanic range of mountains,— which is thus "bulwarked by a quake-distorted range of mountains buried in eternal ice and snow and rearing 10,000 feet into the sky." Behind this barrier rises a veil of vapor, and "twisting fiords penetrate the ragged ice-gnarled coast."

The article further describes some imaginary conditions, which, however, have some scientific foundation, concerning this land and its people:

"Just inside the mountains, hangs a veil of fog, the vapor of contrasting temperatures, for here we may imagine the aspect changes sharply. Heat from a nether world defies the cold. White of snow and ice shades swiftly to the green of verdant pastures and gold of wooded uplands.

---

30. Edward H, Anderson, "Are There a People in the Far North," *Improvement Era*, Vol. 27, pp. 256-257, January, 1924.

"We come upon a level clearing on which are spread symmetrically half a hundred human habitations. Tall men magnificently built and clad in short and bright-hued loosely fitting blouses are moving leisurely about. Mingling with them are comely, fair-haired women in dainty smocks. Laughing children dash here and there among the shrubbery.

"No savages are these descendants of the vanished colony. Indeed, we shall be mistaken if they are not far in advance of our smug selves in culture, learning, deportment, and social refinement. They have harnessed natural energy to an amazing degree. They know the truths of other worlds. They have mastered the secrets of health."

Such a prognostication is indulged in by those who "picture a polar paradise like some Titan emerald in its alabaster setting." (*Improvement Era*, 27:256-257, January 1924.)

Although Anderson did not uphold the theory mentioned in the *Popular Science Monthly*, which he later referred to as only "speculations,"[31] it is interesting to note how structurally similar this theory is to one that was recorded in the diary of Benjamin F. Johnson, published in 1947.[32]

In his diary, Benjamin Johnson attributes a statement to the Prophet Joseph Smith, who this time supposedly said that the Lost Ten Tribes were "in the north pole in a concave just the shape of" a "kettle,"—which shape is similar to the "volcano surrounded center" as expressed in the *Popular Science Monthly* article previously discussed. This account by Johnson has sometimes been called by its supporters,[33] the "main basis" for their belief in the so-called "concave theory." Johnson's diary reads as follows:

I [Johnson] asked where the nine and half tribes of Israel were. "Well," said he [Joseph Smith], "you remember the old caldron or potash kettle you used to boil maple sap in for sugar, don't you?" I said yes. "Well," said he, "they are in the north pole in a concave just the shape of that kettle. And John the Revelator is with them, preparing them for their return."[34]

31. *Ibid.*, p. 257.
32. Benjamin F. Johnson, *My Life's Review,* Zion's Printing & Publishing Company, 1947, p. 93.
33. R. Clayton Brough, "The Hollow Earth Theory," *op. cit.*
34. *Ibid.*

As a sidelight to the above quotation, it is perhaps appropriate to mention here that Benjamin Johnson was not the only member of the Church to relate that the Lost Ten Tribes were possibly in a "concave" area in the North Pole. For in October, 1919, Nephi Anderson, an L.D.S. writer, wrote a fictional story in the *Relief Society Magazine,* which told about a "fictitious person named Lon Merton of Chicago, who supposedly went on a sea voyage in the arctic regions, was separated from the rest of the crew, and found the ten tribes living in a concave surface in an area of the North Pole. The fictitious Merton then states that these people had been visited by Christ nearly 2,000 years ago, who by the time of his (Merton's) visit were still practicing the Saviors teachings. The story ends with an allied airplane making a forced landing nearby, Merton gives the pilot a letter to his relatives back home and also his life's story which he had previously written; whereupon he (Merton) stays at the North Pole and the plane then flies away only to crash again somewhere else, whereupon a crew finds the wrecked plane and Lon Merton's story.[35]

Following the numerous explorations and intensive geographical chartings of the North Pole region by various nations, which began in earnest in the 1920's and has continued to our own day, "not even one 'concave civilization' or 'big hole' was ever discovered."[36]As a result, by the late 1940's the Hollow Earth (or Concave) Theory had lost many of its Latter day Saint adherents.[37] In 1978, this author, after conducting a cross-sectional survey, has found that the percentage of Latter-day Saints who believe in the "Hollow Earth (or Concave) Theory" may now possibly total no more than 4% of those members of the Church who express themselves as having a specific opinion as to where the Lost Ten Tribes may presently be located. This is the lowest percentage rating of any of the four major theories discussed in this book.[38]

The North Pole Theory

The third theory which has been proposed by various Latter-day Saints to explain the present location of the Lost Ten Tribes is the so-called "North Pole Theory." Presently, this theory proposes that

35. Nephi Anderson, "Beyond Arsareth, *Relief Society Magazine,* Vol. 6, pp. 561 ff, October 1919.
36. R. Clayton Brough, "The Hollow Earth Theory," *op. cit.*
37. *Ibid.*
38. R. Clayton Brough, 'Results of a Survey ," *op. cit.*

the Lost Ten Tribes possibly live in a "mysteriously camouflaged" geographical area somewhere at or near the North Pole.

Although at first glance this theory might seem very similar to the "Hollow Earth (or Concave) Theory," since both theories propose that the Lost Ten Tribes are located today in a region either somewhere near, at, or in the North Pole, the difference is that the former theory proposes that the Lost Ten Tribes are in a concave area, like a volcano, or in a *great hollow area*, somewhere in the region of the North Pole, while today the latter theory proposes that the Lost Ten Tribes are hidden by some type of supernatural means in a *mysteriously camouflaged region* somewhere near or at the North Pole.

The North Pole Theory apparently had its beginning in the very early days of the Church. Though it began to circulate in rather simplistic form in about the mid-1800's, and became rather complex by the mid-1900's, it began as early as 1835, when Elder William W. Phelps, who at times acted as a scribe for the Prophet Joseph Smith, made the speculation that possibly "a continent" existed at the North Pole whereupon the Lost Ten Tribes could exist. In a letter to Elder Oliver Cowdery, Elder Phelps stated:

> The parts of the globe that are known probably contain 700 millions of inhabitants, and those parts which are unknown may be supposed to contain more than four times as many more, making an estimated total of about three thousand, five hundred and eighty millions of souls: Let no man marvel at this statement, because there may be a continent at the north pole, of more than 1300 square miles, containing thousands of millions of Israelites, who, after a high way is cast up in the great deep, may come to Zion, singing songs of everlasting joy. The Lord must bring to pass the words of Isaiah, which say to the North "Give up; and to the South; keep not back: bring my sons from far, and my daughters from the ends of the earth." From the north and south end, I presume, as no one has ever pretended, that there was an end to the globe anywhere else.[39]

By the mid-1860's the North Pole Theory had gained considerable respectability among many Church leaders and members. Among those Latter-day Saints who proposed its possibility was Elder Orson Pratt, one of the most profound speakers and prophet-

---

39. W. W. Phelps, "A Letter to Oliver Cowdery." *Messenger & Advocate*, Vol. 2, p. 194, October 1835.

ic Apostles the Church has ever known. However, Elder Pratt did not just limit his lectures and discourses to revealed gospel truths, he also undertook at times to methodically and analytically discuss the possibilities of the unknown. For example, on one occasion in 1867, Elder Pratt took it upon himself to figure out the distance and time that would have been involved for the Lost Ten Tribes to "likely" reach a "land in the neighborhood of the North Pole." He stated:

> When the Ten Tribes left Assyria they crossed the Euphrates River from west to east, miraculously. They must have repented of their sins or God would not have miraculously divided the river for them to pass over. They likely passed between the Black and Caspian Seas and continued on through Russia to the extreme north shores of Europe, i.e., 2500 miles north. But this could not be a year and a half's journey: indeed, it would not be an average of five miles a day. From many intimations of ancient prophecy they evidently had a highway made for them in the midst of the Arctic Ocean and were led to a land in the neighborhood of the North Pole. This region would be about 4000 miles north of their Assyrian residence and could be traveled in eighteen months time at an average of a little less than eight miles a day.[40]

It is perhaps interesting to note, such as in the above statement, that Elder Orson Pratt, when speaking of the North Pole as being the "likely" or "possible" area where the Lost Ten Tribes might be located, always used some type of reserved terminology when speaking of that particular geographical region, such as: "the Ten Tribes . . . were led to a land in the neighborhood of the North Pole" (stated by him in 1867); "and . . . those dreary, desolate, cold arctic regions . . . around the pole" (said in 1875).[41]

Following Elder Pratt's statement of 1867, and several other statements made by him during the next fifteen years, Elder George Reynolds, who served as one of the seven presidents of the First Quorum of Seventy, ventured in 1883, to go beyond Elder Pratt's ideas, and wrote his own views on what the possible "feelings and emotions" of the people of the Lost Ten Tribes might have been "when they stood facing the icy waters of the Arctic Sea." He stated:

> . . . what must have been the sensations of even the boldest when they stood facing the icy waters of the Arctic Sea! . . .

---

40. Orson Pratt, "Where Are The Ten Tribes of Israel?", *Millennial Star*, Vol. 29, pp. 200-201, March 30,1867.

41. Orson Pratt, *Journal of Discourses*, 1875, Vol. 18, pp. 23, 26, 68.

they approach the frozen shores of these unexplored waters in the gloom of the arctic winter's continued night, then their feelings of awe must have been still more intense. No wonder if some turned aside, retraced their steps into northern Europe and mingled the seed of Ephraim with that of the heathen in those parts. But the main body did not falter, they followed where God led, yet farther north. Whether they crossed on the ice of winter, or whether by direct interposition of Jehovah, such as when the waters of the Red Sea were divided, we know not; to learn this secret we must abide His time, when the story of their exodus from Media and establishment in Arsareth will be revealed.[42]

Speculation about the Lost Tribes possibly being somewhere near or at the North Pole continued during the 1880's and 1890's, and apparently reached its peak during the first few years of the 1900's. In fact, so intense was the speculation among various Latter-day Saints, particularly in Utah, that by 1903, the inevitable happened—the first book was published purporting to tell of *"The Discovery of the Ten Tribes as Found in the Arctic Ocean.!"* The book was published by O. J. S. Lindelof of Salt Lake City, who claimed that he obtained the material for the book from a "dying sailer" when he "visited Northern Europe . . . to one of the villages of the sea coast . . . and found a dying man to whom" he "administered and assisted financially, in his dying moments." Lindelof further claimed that the sailor who he administered to "repayed" his "kindness" for the "administration" by giving him a "musty manuscript," which the sailor said he had found "south of Baffin's Bay [located off the southwest coast of Greenland] and which he could not read because it was in "another language." Lindelof then states that to his surprise the unknown "language" was his "own language," and he "was so struck with" the "manuscript" that he "concluded to have it published as quickly as" he "returned to America, and could copy it." He further added that upon reading the manuscript, which "was written on poor paper; in fact it looked more like tissue paper than anything else, and it must also have been penetrated by salt water, for it was in a bad shape and quite hard to decipher," that the manuscript told of a "whaling ship" named the "Mt. Walston,[43]

---

42. George Reynolds, "The Assyrian Captivity," *Juvenille Instructor*, Vol. 18, p. 28, January 15, 1883.

43. O. J. S. Lindelof, *A Trip to the North Pole, or the Discovery of the Ten Tribes as Found in the Arctic Ocean*, Tribune Printing Company, Salt Lake City, Utah, 1903, pp. 1-17, 197-199. *Note:* The author, after considerable research, could not verify the existence of a whaling ship named the "Mt. Walston."

commanded by Captain E. F. Nye, which "left San Francisco in 1879," and "was never heard from again;" except that one of the crewmen on board the vessel, Joe B. Lothare, a "boat steerer," managed to survive long enough to write down (and later "seal them up" in a bottle) the events which betell him and a few of his other shipmates before the Mt. Walston sank somewhere in the region of the North Pole.

What follows are a few excerpts from Lindelof's book. which were supposedly "originally written" by "boat steerer" Joe B. Lothare, describing the events that befell the Mt. Walston and its crew, as well as the discovery by some of its crewmen of the "Lost Ten Tribes," who supposedly then inhabited the "North Pole Continent." Even if the following account may not be factual, it is at least entertaining:

In the year 1879. a whaling ship left San Francisco which was named the Mt. Walston, commanded by Captain Nye.

Like a great many others that had left before him, he was never heard from again; and his ship, like others. was lost to the civilized world, but not to the writer, who had the satisfaction of drifting with the ship, by way of Behring strait east of Wrangle island north by northeast into the unexplored regions of the Arctic ocean.

We were in a *lead* which we followed one hundred and twenty-five miles, when it opened up like a halfmoon on either side with the lead still open to the front of us.

We had scarcely sailed within eight or ten lengths of the vessel when the lead closed up in front and looking back we perceived that the same thing had occurred in the rear. The reader can readily see that we were incased in a circle of ice, making an Arctic ocean in miniature. As we drifted north-by-east, the ice closed in upon the vessel, so that we could leave the ship for the main floe, which we found to be a vast field of ice.

The ship drifted along with the floe for many days, when we heard in front of us a thundering, crunching, popping sound, which continued for several days, and seemed to be getting nearer and nearer. During most of this time it had been snowing, with an occasional sleet and rain, which froze on the spars and ropes, and gave the ship the appearance of being studded with diamonds, as the beautiful Aurora Borealis shed its bleaching light over our surroundings. Many were the thoughts of home and friends as the boats were lowered and provided with the necessary paraphernalia for our journey. We had taken the precaution to procure dogs and sleds from the natives, for certain personal property, belonging to the vessel; in case that any accident should happen, which we momentarily were expecting from the noises in front. This noise, however, proved to be the ice breaking up.

By way of introduction, I will introduce the ship's crew, which will be found in full at the end of the record. As I stated, the Mt. Walston was commanded by Capt. Nye. There were five mates and about thirty-four sailors, one cook, assisted by two Chinese cooks whom we had taken on board after leaving San Francisco to assist Huder; and [I,] a young adventurer by the name of J. B. Lothare, whose sole object was to study nature in its wildest aspects.

Captain Nye, Lothare and twenty seamen were well ensconced in two boats, while the other seamen and Chinese cooks were in two other boats. The dogs were equally divided, with a sled in each boat. While the boat with the Chinese in was the first prepared, and by its crew of sailors taken upon the hummocky ice, ours was barely lowered by the side of the ship on the new ice, when the great shock came at last. The shock was caused by the west part of the lead, which extended further ahead than the east part, striking a promontory of an unknown island to the northwest of us, thus opening wide the lead in front, with an open sea to the north. This left our ship free and easy on a smooth and open sea.

We are not slow in availing ourselves of the opportunity of clambering into our vessel and putting up our boats. But what had become of the other boats? In the commotion they had been engulfed between two ice bergs, and seven brave men were lost from our party.

Having discovered two polar bears, two of the men had followed them, and one man with the two Chinese, dogs and sleds, had followed after to bring back the game. They were gracefully floating on a detached piece of ice, when we lowered a boat and relieved them from their perilous position.

We were all thankful for the safety of our Chinese cooks, as there was not one of us who could superintend the culinary department except Huder. We spent the remainder of the day in thanking God for the safety of our crew and ship, and also asking for His mercy for our departed friends. Our thoughts were again turned to our own future.

We could now see a solid bank of ice behind us and an open sea to the north of us, and it dawned on more than one man on board this vessel that we were nearing the North Pole, never to return from whence we came. At least these were my thoughts.

Wonders will never cease. We had been traveling through a temperature of one hundred and five to one hundred and ten below freezing point, when now, within two hundred miles of the North Pole, we found a climate comparatively mild, and the nearer we approached to the Pole, the milder was our climate. The Aurora Borealis, or Northern light. seemed to give out a light and warmth that we had not before experienced.

I had long believed that the Pole was surrounded by a belt of ice, that, if it could be penetrated, would discover an open sea,

but now my idea was virtually established. Should I ever be able to enlighten the scientific world in regard to the matter?

We were now within one hundred miles of the North Pole, and began to discover coast fowl. Can any human conceive the thought that passed through our minds on the possibility of discovering a probably inhabited Polar region?

We were now sailing at a good pace when the watch called out, "Land Ahead."

All was bustle and excitement. We had discovered the North Pole.

There was no questioning the fact. Ducks and geese were seen as we progressed toward the North. What! Why there were actually boats manned by white people like ourselves! Had we arrived at some European port? No; for when our ship approached, the boats fled before us into a beautiful harbor surrounded by a magnificent city, built after the style of ancient cities of six to eight hundred years B.C.

We landed in this capacious harbor and were received by what seemed to be a delegation of officials. But, although we spoke several languages, we were not able to understand the men. They were dressed in loose costumes, something after the Persian style. They seemed very white, with a delicate transparency of feature.

We were led to different buildings, through signs and gestures, and after leaving the ship in charge of some of the men, Capt. Nye, First Mate Linder (or Day), Second Mate Jost (or Omey), two seamen and myself, (may I venture to introduce myself as the adventurous J. B. Lothare?) We followed our guide, but took the precaution to take our rifles, pistols and other weapons along.

After leaving our boat we landed on a well-made dock, paved with a sort of brown slate rock. We passed into a street paved with the same material and to my surprise the houses were all built of well-burned brick.

But I must say that we found out afterwards there must be no more surprises, for we had actually found the ten lost tribes of Israel, who were sent to the northwestern part of Asia, and from there sent into the north country. We read in First Kings, XIV Chapter and XV Verse:

"For the Lord shall smite Israel as a reed is shaken in the water, and He shall root up Israel out of this good land which he gave to the fathers, and shall scatter them beyond the river," etc., etc.

We read also in Second Kings, XVIII Chapter, that the King of Assyria, Shalmenenezer, did remove the children of Israel out of the Lord's sight. There was none left but the tribes of Judah, (XXIII Verse).

I referred to my Bible, to investigate if perchance this might not be the Ten Tribes of Israel, and I shall at least call them so, from all these Bible readings and also on account of other information. I have gleaned this from their customs and habits, and from certain traditions which coincided with other descriptive customs of ancient Israel. They spoke the old Hebrew language, which I afterwards learned, as I was delegated to study their language.

But to return to my narrative. We were lead into what appeared to be a spacious palace. After crossing the court, we were ushered into this palace by liveried servants, and at last were brought before a beautiful lady on a throne decorated with all the paraphernalia pertaining to so dignified a position. It seems that our approach had been heralded to the Queen, who this actually was, and who had ascended her throne for the purpose of finding out our mission, and also hoping that we might be deliverers of her people. For they had an ancient tradition that some day they should be brought out from that land by some person and taken to a land from whence their forefathers had been driven.

The Queen had barely passed her honeymoon with King Manasherous, when the King had lost his life in making a raid on the island stronghold of a vicious and daring robber band, who had been strengthened by refugees from justice and all manner of outlaws, . . .

Then, 181 pages later, we read:

I am now needed to steer . . . and therefore must close my record. If we go through you will see us, but if we fail, you will find the records, for we expect to land in Baffin's Bay and there throw out the records after sealing them up. If we fail to reach safety, good-bye! In God I trust!

Now, I proceed to seal up the records. May God deliver it to some one who will give it to the civilized world, if I fail to reach it myself. Again, good-bye! I may not see you, but I will surely, through the grace of Christ Jesus, see my dear wife, Leta."

[See footnote 43 of this chapter]

Although this author has not been able to determine if Lindelof's book played any significant part in increasing the speculation among Latter-day Saints that the Lost Ten Tribes might possibly be located somewhere near or at the North Pole, it does not matter; for the speculation that was then so prevalent, soon began to subside when a few years later scientific exploration of the North Pole region began taking place.[44]

In 1909, when Admiral Robert E. Peary led a successful expedition to the north geographic pole, his "discovery" that it was "uninhabited" caused some serious consternation among a number of Latter-day Saints, who were "sure" that he would find the "Lost Ten Tribes." Recognizing the problems that some Latter-day Saints had placed themselves in by believing that a "theory" was a "fact," the General Authorities of the Church began speaking out on the "fact" that the "loose teaching" which had been "spread around" that the Lost Ten Tribes had settled in the region(s) of the North Pole was not Church doctrine.[45]

For example, on November 4, 1909, a few months following Admiral Peary's "discovery," President Charles W. Penrose, then an Apostle, wrote in the *Millennial Star* the following caution to the Latter-day Saints:

. . . "The north" has been mentioned both in ancient and modern lands as a place where Israel would be gathered from, and this has led to the notion, entertained by some persons, that the lost tribes were located somewhere in the neighborhood of

---

44. Walt Whipple, *op. cit.*, pp. 14-16.
45. *Ibid.*

the north pole. This has not been an established doctrine of the Church, but simply a theory that has been deduced out of some of the saying of the prophets.[46]

Within one year after writing the statement mentioned on page 70 for the *Millennial Star,* President Penrose again wrote another statement, which this time appeared in the *Improvement Era* of October, 1910. In this article he explained that the exact whereabouts of the Lost Ten Tribes of Israel had not been confirmed by revelation. He also added that the vast areas in the arctic region had not yet been fully explored, thereby not excluding the possibility of the existence of the Lost Ten Tribes being "near" the North Pole, if such should later prove true:

> . . . some people have imagined they were in the neighborhood of the north pole, and since the alleged "discoveries" of that region by Commander Peary and, perhaps, Dr. Cook, they have felt somewhat disappointed, feeling compelled to abandon the idea. Now, in the first place, there has been no positive *revelation* or *authoritative* announcement that the Ten Tribes existed in a separate body at or near the north pole. In the next place, the explorations and developments concerning the polar region have been chiefly conducted from points on the American continent, while the vast regions northward from the eastern hemisphere have been comparatively unexplored. It is quite possible, therefore, that there may be lands and peoples, in the extreme north of the other half of the globe, which are yet undiscovered and unknown . . . .[47]

A few years later, in 1919, Elder Hyrum M. Smith, an Apostle, and Janne M. Sjodahl, an LDS author, published the *Doctrine and Covenants Commentary,* wherein they expressed that even though "Peary discovered the Pole . . . the Lord can . . . keep (the lost tribes) hidden from the knowledge of others, until the time comes for the revelation to be made known, wherever they are."

A great many skeptical people rejoiced when the announcement was made that Commodore Peary had discovered the North Pole, and they declared that this proved beyond a doubt that the lost tribes were not in the north. The Lord never said that they were at the North Pole. No matter whether Commodore Peary discovered the Pole or not, there is a great deal of country in the north that no man, to our knowledge has visited. The fact

---

46. Charles W. Penrose, *Millennial Star,* Vol. 71, p. 699, November 4, 1909.
47. Charles W. Penrose, *Improvement Era,* Vol. 13, p. 1087; October, 1910.

remains that the Lord can take care of these people and keep them hidden from the knowledge of others, until the time comes for the Revelation to be made known, wherever they are. A highway shall be cast up in the midst of the sea and the ice shall flow down at their presence, when the time comes for their journey to Zion. It shall no longer be said, "the Lord liveth that brought up the children of Israel out of the land of Egypt; but the Lord liveth, that brought up the children of Israel from the land of the north." (Jer.16:14-15), so great shall be the miracle of their deliverance. (D&C 133:26-34)[48]

In January 1924, the Editor of the *Improvement Era*, in an article entitled: "Are There a People in the Far North?" expressed that:
     In one of the revelations in the Doctrine and Covenants, (Section 133:26-34) we are told that they who are in the North country shall come in remembrance before the Lord and their prophets shall hear his voice and shall no longer stay themselves; "and they shall smite the rocks and the ice shall flow down at their presence." The North has been mentioned both in ancient and modern times as a place from which should be gathered Israel, and this had led to the understanding sometimes held that the Lost tribes were located somewhere in the neighborhood of the North Pole. It should be understood that this is not a doctrine of the Church, but simply a theory that has been entertained and based upon the sayings of the prophets of Israel. However, the above quotation in the 133rd section of the Doctrine and Covenants is perhaps the most pertinent revelation concerning the location of the tribes in the north. This reference is in harmony with the predictions of the ancient prophets of Israel, and refers, as one may see plainly, to the body of people descended from the remnant of Israel, called the "lost tribes."[49]
Following this *Improvement Era* article of January, 1924, so many scientific investigations of the North Pole and its surrounding lands were undertaken that the North Pole Theory had lost most of its supporters by the 1940's.[50]

---

48. Hyrum M. Smith & Janne M. Sjodahl, *Doctrine & Covenants Commentary*, Deseret Book Company, 1974, p. 844.
     49 Editor, *Improvement Era*, Vol. 27, pp. 256-260, January 1924.
     50. R. Clayton Brough, "Results of a Survey . . . .," *op. cit. Note:* President Joseph Fielding Smith said in 1942: "Somebody will come along and say, 'Brother Smith, they [the Lost Ten Tribes] cannot be in the north country because men have been up to the North Pole.' I did not say they were up at the North Pole. The Lord has not said they were up at the North Pole. I don't know where they are. If I did, they would not be lost." (Joseph Fielding Smith. *The Signs ot the Times*, Deseret News Press. Salt Lake City, Utah, 1942, p. 42.)

In 1926, Admiral Richard E. Byrd and Floyd Bennett of the United States reached the north geographical pole by airplane; and within the next twenty years the polar ice cap had been so thoroughly explored and charted that there seemed little hope left for anyone to further believe in the theory.

In 1958, the U.S.S. Nautilus became the first submarine to pass under the Arctic ice to the north geographical pole, and this about ended any support for either the North Pole Theory or the Hollow Earth (or Concave) Theory.

Recently, however, with the increase in such speculative phenomena as the "Bermuda Triangle, U.F.O.'s, Bigfoot, and the Loch Ness Monster," the North Pole Theory seems to be taking on another type of "believable dimension" among a few Latter-day Saints.[51] The reason? Because some Latter-day Saints now support the "possibility" that the Lost Ten Tribes are "hidden from the rest of mankind somewhere in the region of the north pole" through the "divine use" of "invisible" or "mysteriously camouflaged techniques, such as through "unknown time-space warps," other "dimensions of time," or "atmospheric-covers of some type." However, even with this added twist, the North Pole Theory still appears to have relatively few supporters among Latter-day Saints today.[52]

The Dispersion Theory

The Fourth theory which has been proposed by Latter-day Saints to explain the present whereabouts of the Lost Ten Tribes is the so-called "Dispersion Theory." This theory, which today seems to be the most popular among the general membership of the Church,[53] proposes that the Lost Ten Tribes have been totally scattered among the present nations of the earth, and are only lost as to their identity—not as to their location, and that they are presently being gathered into the Church through missionary labors.

What makes this particular theory so different from the others, and so unusual in its acceptance by Latter-day Saints, is that it proposes that the Lost Ten Tribes are "entirely or totally scattered among the present nations of the earth," which directly conflicts with the united teachings of past and present General Authorities

---

51. *Ibid.* (Conversations with some Latter-day Saints even raised the suggestion that U.F.O's or ' Flying Saucers" are controlled by people who belong to the Lost Ten Tribes.")

52. R. Clayton Brough, Results of a Survey . . . ." *op. cit.*, see p. 42, footnote number 5.

53. *Ibid.*

who have stated that "at least a sufficient number or large portion of the Lost Ten Tribes are today united together as one body or group of people, whose present location is unknown to mankind."[54] In addition, while the other three previously described theories are basically derived from the personal "opinions or views" of various General Authorities of the Church, the Dispersion Theory is based upon the writings and scriptural interpretations of a few Latter-day Saints within the general membership of the Church.[55]

To begin with, as far as this author has been able to determine, the Dispersion Theory may have first had its beginning among Latter-day Saints in the early 1900's. In 1912, Elder Brigham H. Roberts, one of the First Seven Presidents of the Quorum of Seventy, stated that "it would have been quite possible for God to scatter . . . [and] to lose these [ten] tribes of Israel among the nations of the earth."[56] Three years prior to 1912, the north pole had been explored by Peary and Cook, and since that period of time, as Elder Roberts states, the Church had been assailed by "local newspaper critics" for its members "alleged belief . . . about the existence of the ten tribes" being "somewhere in the polar regions." In 1912, Elder Roberts, refuted this "alleged belief" of the local newspaper critics, by stating that

> In none of the revelations of God is there any expression that would lead one to believe that God had located the ten tribes about the north pole . . . . but this I believe, for myself, that within the known regions of the earth, where the children of men are located, it is quite possible for God to fulfill all his predictions in relation to the return of Israel. It would have been quite possible for God to scatter, or to use the language of the prophet Amos—"Sift the house of Israel among all nations, like as corn is sifted in a sieve," and "yet not the least grain fall upon the Earth"—i.e. not be lost to the knowledge of God, though now lost to men."[57]

The following is a fuller text of Elder Roberts' comments:

---

54 See Chapter Two of this book.

55. R. Clayton Brough, " Results of a Survey . ." *op. cit;* Walt Whipple. *op. cit.,* pp. 20-21.

56. Brigham H. Roberts, *Defense of the Faith and the Saints, op cit.,* Vol. 2, pp. 447-480.

57. *Ibid.*

I have observed some criticisms in our local press in relation to the views entertained by the Latter-day Saints about the return of the lost tribes of Israel from the land of the north. We have recently had the north pole discovered—well, discovered twice, if reports be true. And it is claimed by the aforesaid local press that the Church entertains the view that somewhere, in this frozen region of the pole these lost tribes have lived, and that it has been the hope of the Latter-day Saints that from the north pole regions these lost tribes would return to supplement them in numbers and power and influence here in this land of our Zion. There is more or less of merriment indulged in because, now that the north pole has been discovered, lo, there is no people there and no place for a people. Ice fields, ice mountains, ice floes, with accompanying desolation—an absolute loneliness out there at the pole! Well, I think men for some time have been sufficiently close to the pole to lead any thoughtful person to the conclusion that such conditions of lonely desolation must have existed there, rather than any continent of salubrious climate and fertile soils, where a great people could be located. Let me offer this suggestion: If those of us who believe in the messages from God given in these last days are likely, because of inability to assess these messages at their full value—if we are likely to have misapprehension of the messages and the purposes of God, certainly those who have no sympathy with them, and who do not believe in them are apt to have still wider misapprehension of the messages and purposes of God. That being true, it is possible also that our local newspaper critics have formed misconceptions concerning an alleged belief of ours about the existence of the ten tribes somewhere in polar regions. I do not know how many Latter-day Saints may have entertained the view that about the polar regions were located the lost tribes of Israel. I do not know how many even of our students—the students of the gospel of this dispensation of the fulness of times—may have entertained the same view. There is the statement of Esdras that there was a year and a half's journey northward from Assyria, by the ten tribes; and there is the promise repeated frequently in Jewish Scriptures, that the Lord would lead back from the north the tribes of Israel. From these statements, some of our people may have concluded that necessarily these lost tribes must be established in the extreme northern portions of the earth, hence the region of the north pole. There may be something in our literature to that effect—I cannot say positively, because I have not had the opportunity, recently, to examine our literature with reference to that particular view. But of this I am positive; that in none of the revelations of God is there any expression that would lead one to believe that God had located the ten tribes about the north pole. The revelations of the Lord do not necessarily lead us to any such conclusion. When the Savior was in the western hemisphere, ministering among the Nephites, he called their attention to the announcement that he had made to his disciples in Judea, when he said, "Other sheep have I which are not of this fold; them also I must bring and they shall hear my voice, and there shall be one fold and one shepherd." (John 10:16.) When ministering to the Nephites, I say, the Messiah explained to them that they were the "other sheep" he had in mind in this passage. Some of the disciples, he explained, believed that he had in mind the gentiles, not appreciating the fact that his manifestation of himself and of his truth to the gentiles should be through the manifestations of the Holy Ghost, rather than by ministration of himself personally to them. The disciples in Judea then had a misapprehension of this matter, though Jesus himself had said that he was not sent (personally) but to the lost sheep of the house of Israel. (Matt. 15:24.) Here, then, in this western world, were the "other sheep," that the Christ had in mind in this remarkable statement that he made to his disciples in Judea. The Messiah also informed the Nephites that he had not only fulfilled this Scripture but now there was still another mission that had been given him, namely to visit the lost tribes of the house of Israel, and manifest himself to them, for though these tribes were lost unto the children of men they were not lost unto the Father. He knew their location, and had given commission to his Son to minister unto them. (See III Nephi, chaps. 15, 16, 17.) But there is nothing in the statement of the Messiah to the Nephites that would compel us to believe that these lost tribes were located about the north pole; but merely expressions in the Scriptures that would lead one to conclude that they were located in northern lands. Then again, in the matter of this return of the "lost tribes of Israel," there are those I believe, who, seeing that there was small hope of a location for them about the north pole, have held that perhaps the said lost tribes were located upon some detached portion of the earth. As to that. 1 have no opinion to express; but *this I believe, for myself,* that within the known regions of the earth, where the children of men are located, it is quite possible for God to fulfill all his predictions in relation to the return of Israel. It would have been quite possible for God to scatter, or to use the language of the prophet Amos—"Sift the house of Israel among all nations, like as corn is sifted in a sieve," and "yet not the least grain fall upon the earth"—i.e. be lost to the knowledge of God, though now lost to men. And as it was possible to lose these tribes of Israel among the nations of the earth, so is it possible for God to recover them from their scattered condition from among these nations, with a display of the divine power.[58]

Nine months after Elder Roberts had published his statement on the "possibility" of the Lord "scattering" or "sifting" the "house of Israel among all nations," Stephen Malan, an L.D.S. writer, printed (in the latter part of 1912) a small book entitled: *The Ten Tribes, Discovered and Identified.* Whether Malan was "inspired" by Elder Roberts comments on the "possible . . . (etc.)," is not known. What is recognized, however, is that for the first time the basic premises of the Dispersion Theory were introduced in published form by an LDS member to the rest of the membership of the Church. In addition, although Malan's book has been criticized for its "shallow research . . . in that he attempted to prove a topic not on the basis of positive evidence against previous theories, but on the basis of a lack of evidence to disprove the theory he was advancing," it did pave the way later for the publication of other similar books.[59]

In his book, it is perhaps interesting to observe that Malan personally interpreted many scriptures which applied to the return of the Lost Ten Tribes quite differently than what was and now is accepted by the Authorities of the Church, relative to their correct and appropriate meaning. For example: in 3 Nephi 17:4, where the Savior, then resurrected, stated: "But now I go unto the Father, and also to show myself unto the lost tribes of Israel, for they are not lost unto the Father, for he knoweth whither he hath taken them," Malan stated his belief that the Lord "gave no hint" as to when this visit was to be made, and therefore he (Malan) believed this promised visit of the Lord to the Lost Ten Tribes was "fulfilled in the Lord's appearance in this dispensation to Joseph Smith."[60]

In contrast to Malan's interpretation of this scripture, Elder Bruce R. McConkie, an Apostle, has stated: "The resurrected Lord

58. *Ibid.*

59. Stephen Malan, *The Ten Tribes, Discovered & Identified*, E.A.L. Scoville Press, Salt Lake City, Utah, 1912, pp. 141-142. Walt Whipple, *op. cit.*, pp. 20-21.

visited and ministered among them (the Lost Ten Tribes) following his ministry on this (American) continent among the Nephites."[61]

In another instance, Malan interpreted the scripture in the Doctrine and Covenants, section 110:11, which reads "After this vision closed the heavens were again opened unto us; and Moses appeared before us, and committed unto us the keys of the gathering of Israel from the four parts of the earth, and the leading of the ten tribes from the land of the north," as meaning the following:

> In my opinion the meaning of this would be clearer if it read something like this: The keys of the gathering and leading of Israel from the land of the north and from all other lands. Otherwise the expression would lead one to think there were two separate people, one by the name of Israel to be gathered from the four parts of the earth, and another called the ten tribes to be led in a body somewhere in the north.[62]

Needless to say, the latter part of Malan's above statement, which mentions two "separate" groups of "people," and which he rejects, is exactly the interpretation that the Brethren of the Church have continually preached.[63] Regarding Malan's above interpretation of D&C 110:11, Walt Whipple has commented as follows:

> [Malan] stated that he felt he had disproved that this scripture could not have a meaning of two different gatherings as many had supposed. After reading this interpretation and comment, I was reminded of the rebutle by George Reynolds of Messrs. Remy and Brechley's criticism on the translation of the papyrus of Abraham made by the Prophet Joseph Smith. They obtained from a scholar by the name of Deveria his opinion as to the meaning of the characters on the facsimilies. Deveria's approach was to alter a figure or character and then tell what it would mean if it was so changed. Reynolds' wit is revealed in the following story:
>
> . . . This puts us in mind of a little story. A certain clergyman was visiting the home of one of his parishioners, when he noticed a little son of his host very busily engaged, first intently eyeing him and then working away at a slate he held in his hand. Suspecting what he was doing, the clergyman asked the boy if he was not drawing his portrait, and finding his suspicions

60. *Ibid.*
61. Bruce R. McConkie, *op. cit.,* p. 457.
62 Stephen Malan, *op. cit.,* p. 153.
63. Walt Whipple, *op. cit.,* pp. 21-22. Also, see Chapter Two of this book.

were correct, he asked to see it. With some reluctance the boy consented. After looking at it a moment, the clergyman exclaimed: "Why, this is not like me!" and received in reply the very consoling answer, "Well, I guess it's not; suppose I put a tail on it and call it a dog." So M. Deveria wants to put a head or a tail on some of these characters and then call them Osiris, Anubis, or some other God! Anything to beat revelation.[64]

In addition, Malan added another interesting personal interpretation of prophetic scripture; this time it was *Doctrine & Covenants*, section 133, verses 26-33, which read as follows:

> And they who are in the north countries shall come in remembrance before the Lord; and their prophets shall hear his voice, and shall no longer stay themselves; and they shall smite the rocks, and the ice shall flow down at their presence.
>
> And an highway shall be cast up in the midst of the great deep.
>
> Their enemies shall become a prey unto them,
>
> And in the barren deserts there shall come forth pools of living water; and the parched ground shall no longer be a thirsty land.
>
> And they shall bring forth their rich treasures unto the children of Ephraim, my servants.
>
> And the boundaries of the everlasting hills shall tremble at their presence.
>
> And there shall they fall down and be crowned with glory, even in Zion, by the hands of the servants of the Lord, even the children of Ephraim.
>
> And they shall be filled with songs of everlasting joy.

And Malan's interpretation of the above scripture:

> The presiding authorities of our modern church in their succession are the only prophets the ten tribes have . . . . But how shall the rocks be smitten and the ice flow down at their coming? Leaving out all consideration of the supernatural, we may say that the most reasonable explanation of this phenomenon lies in the skillful engineering, the explosives, the machinery, the manual labor expended in the construction of our railroads over the plains, mountain defiles, across rivers and through mountains. And no doubt, too, this work in the rocks would affect the ice-bound regions of the north.[65]

---

64. *Ibid.*
65. Stephen Malan. *op. cit.*, pp. 144,162.

Thus it seems that Malan, at least for himself, was able to solve the entire problem of the return of the Lost Ten Tribes from the "north countries" in the Last Days, by simply interpreting the applicable scriptures in such a manner that "the Latter-day Saints who are now gathering to Zion fulfill all the prophecies on the return of the Lost Ten Tribes."[66]

Although Malan was apparently the first Latter-day Saint writer to present in published form the basic premises of the Dispersion Theory, he is not generally considered the real "father" of the theory. Instead, that honor goes to James H. Anderson, an LDS author and prominent historian. The reason Anderson is considered the "father" of the Dispersion Theory is because he was the first Latter-day Saint to expound the theory with such great reasoning, logic, and scriptural ability that he was often able to place other Latter-day Saints on the defensive because of their own beliefs in any of the other three theories.[67] In fact, it is Anderson who is credited for stating that the Lost Ten Tribes are today entirely scattered among the present nations of the earth, and are only lost as to their identity—not as to their location. . . ."[68] For example, in his book: *God's Covenant Race*, published in 1938, Anderson stated that:

> I have just one suggestion to offer: . . . Let us . . . get fixed in our minds the one fact of the Bible, Book of Mormon and Doctrine and Covenants, that the Ten Tribes were lost only as to their identity and not as to their location, which has always been given as the "north countries" and the "Isles of the sea." The Lord has now begun to reveal their identity, first with the tribe of Ephraim, and then with the other tribes, when the time comes.[69]

In addition to using Malan's earlier technique of personally interpreting scriptures, Anderson also quoted two of the General Authorities of the Church, whose statements he felt upheld his view that the Lost Ten Tribes were "entirely scattered" throughout the nations of the world, and were therefore only "lost as to their identity, and not as to their location."[70] These two Brethren that Anderson quoted were President Brigham Young, and Elder Anthony W. Ivins, an Apostle who later served as first counselor to President Heber J. Grant. The statements of these two General

---

66. Walt Whipple. *op. cit.*, p. 22.
67. Walt Whipple. *op. cit.*, pp. 22-23.
68. James H. Anderson, *op. cit.*, p. 128.
69. *Ibid.*
70. Walt Whipple, *op. cit.*, pp. 22-23.

Authorities, which Anderson quotes in support of his above viewpoint, are as follows:

Brigham Young: The sons of Ephraim are wild and uncultivated, unruly, ungovernable. The spirit in them is turbulent and resolute; they are the Anglo–Saxon race, and they are upon the face of the whole earth, bearing the spirit of rule and dictation, to go forth from conquering to conquer.

Anthony W. Ivins: The thought is becoming almost universal in the British Isles that Israel is there, where we have always known them to be.[71]

What Anderson fails to quote however, are some of the preceding and following comments that President Young and Elder Ivins stated, which help to clarify the meaning of the statements quoted above. For example, President Young stated just prior to his above remark that: "We are now gathering the children of Abraham who have come through the loins of Joseph and his sons, more especially through Ephraim, whose children are mixed among all nations of the earth."[72] And Elder Ivins later stated: "I have not at any time said that there might not be representatives of the ten tribes hidden away of whose existence we have no knowledge, but I do say without hesitation, that they exist in great numbers among the people of Northern Europe, and particularly in the British Isles and the Scandinavian countries."[73] Hence, from these additional statements, it appears that instead of Anderson's viewpoint, that President Young and Elder Ivins are in agreement with other General Authorities of the Church, who have consistently and unitedly stated that the reason "so much of the blood of Ephraim has been found hidden and unknown in the midst of the nations of northern Europe" is because as the Lost Ten Tribes journeyed northward "some of the backsliding Israel (particularly those people of the tribes of Ephraim) rebelled, turned aside from the main body, forgot their God, and by and by mingled with the Gentiles and became the leaven to leaven with the promised seed all the nations of the earth."[74]

Regarding this teaching that "some" of the people who belonged to the Lost Ten Tribes "turned aside from the main body" and later

71. Brigham Young, *Journal of Discourses*, Vol. 10, p.188. Anthony W. Ivins, *Conference Report*, October 3, 1926.

72. Brigham Young, *Journal of Discourses*, Vol. 10, p. 188.

73. Anthony W. Ivins, *The Lost Tribes, op. cit.*, pp.14-15.

74. See Chapter Two of this book.

"mingled with the Gentiles . . . to leaven . . . all the nations of the earth, "Elder Ivins has written that some of the "representatives of the [lost ten] tribes of Israel moved on in a northwesterly direction until they reached Denmark," and that "the great majority" of the Anglo Saxon people of Europe are "descended from the ten tribes":

During the reign of Hosea. King of Israel, Shalmaneser, King of Assyria, carried the ten tribes captive and planted them in Halah, and Habor, on the river Gozen in the cities of the Medes. This country was on the upper reaches of the Tigris and Euphrates rivers. Traveling northwesterly from this point would take them on the west side of the Caucasus Mountains, and on the east of the Black Sea. It is on the northwest coast of the Black Sea that the country known as the Russian Crimea, one of the most productive and delightful parts of the known world, is situated.

At this point three rivers empty into the Black Sea, the names of which are very suggestive—the Danube, the Daneister, and the Danisper. [Supposedly named after the tribe of "Dan"] The river Sereth empties into the Danube, just before the latter reaches the sea. The most direct evidence however that we have that the Crimea was occupied by the ten tribes is the fact that many burial places have been opened there, which prove beyond doubt that the people interred in that particular locality were of Israelitish descent.

Professor Chowlson of the National Museum of St. Petersburg, tells us that he has examined no less than 700 tombstones, and 150 other epigraphs, all of which are in Hebrew, that have been taken from these burials of which the following are a few examples:

"This is the tomb stone of Buki, the Priest. May his rest be in Eden, at the time of the salvation of Israel. Rabbi Moses Levi died in the year of our exile 726. Zadoc, the Levite, son of Moses, died 4000 years after the creation, 785 of our exile. To one of the faithful in Israel, Abraham-Nar-Sinohah, or Kortch, in the year of our exile 1682. when the envoys of the prince of Rosh Meshec from Kiow came to our master, Chazar, Prince David, Halaah, Habor, Gozan, to which place Tiglath Pileser had exiled the sons of Reuben and Gad, and the half tribe of Menasseh, and permitted to settle there, and from which time they have been scattered throughout the entire west, even as far as China.

"I am Jehudi, the son of Moses, the son of Jehudah, the mighty, a man of the tribe of Napthali, of the family of Shim, who was carried captive in the captivity of Hosen, king of Israel, with the tribe of Simeon, together with other tribes of Israel."

From the Crimea representatives of the tribes of Israel moved on in a northwesterly direction until they reached Denmark, Dan's land, and the British Isles where they were amalgamated with the people who had previously reached that country by way of the Mediterranean Sea.

The dictionaries tell us that the word "Saxon" is derived from Saere, a short sword, or long knife. D. W. Holt Yates says: "The word Saxon comes from the sons of Isaac."

There are known to be millions of people in Russia who are the descendants of Abraham, and the tribes of Israel.

This letter is already long, and but a fraction of the evidence that the Anglo Saxon people of Europe are—not all of course, but the great majority—people descended from the ten tribes. The evidence is so convincing that I cannot doubt it.[75]

And President Charles W. Penrose has likewise stated:

There is no doubt in the minds of those who have investigated this subject, that when traveling northward, as described in Esdras, the tribes of Israel mingled on the way with Gentile nations, and that numbers of their posterity are to be found in the various provinces of Germany, in Switzerland, in Holland, in

---

75. Anthony W Ivins, *The Lost Tribes, op. cit,* pp. 9-15. *Note:* Elder George Reynolds, quoting the *Encyclopedia Britannica.* has similarly written: On entering on these ancient books (of Scandinavia) we are immediately struck with the corroborative evidence which they furnish of the eastern origin of the Goths, the fathers of the Scandinavians. As all languages, so all mythologies run in lines, which converge in one common center. . . Central Asia. And little as we might expect it, no sooner do we open the ancient religious books of Scandinavia than we are carried back thither. Our northern people are a people of eastern origin. [The Saxon kings traced themselves back to Odin, who was traced back in his descent from David, as may be seen in a very ancient manuscript in the Herald's College of London.] Odin and his Asar, are Asiatics, declare themselves to be from the great Svithiod, a country which appears to have been the present Circassia, lying between the Black and Caspian Seas. The whole of their memoirs abounded with the proofs of it. They brought with them abundant eastern customs, those of burning the dead, and burying under mounds. They practiced polygamy, looked back with imperishable affection to the great Svithiod, to the primitive district of Asgord and the city of Gudahem or the homes of the gods. They transferred a religion bearing the primal features of those of Persia, India and Greece, to the snowy mountains of Scandinavia." In reading the above we were strongly impressed with the geographical idea there expressed. Without any great stretch of the imagination we could easily consider the traditions regarding the great Svithiod, to refer to Media, the primitive district of Asgord, to be the dim remembrance of their first home in the land of promise, and Gudahem, the home of the gods to be Jerusalem, the city of the great King. The parallel we consider to be very significant. (George Reynolds. *Are We of Israel,. . .* pp. 41-42.)

Sweden, Denmark, Norway, Finland, Iceland, and the numerous islands in the far north.

Much of the blood of Israel is doubtless, to be found in the British Isles. It was obtained, in all probability, by the admixture of Saxon, Danish, Norwegian and Swedish blood with that of the ancient Britons and the Picts and Scots, who inhabited those islands and were subject to the incursions and conquests of the people mentioned, among whose ancestors the Israelites mingled in their journey of a year and a half towards the extreme north. Thus the nations here mentioned became impregnated with the seed of Israel, and their descendants who came to this country, bringing the principles of religious freedom and planting the standard of liberty, were also of the lineage to whom many blessings were promised, and from among all these, many who are of Israel embrace the gospel of the latter-day dispensation. The gathering of some of their descendants to Zion is in part fulfillment of the prophecies in regard to the gathering, but there are revelations [D&C 133:26-34] which cannot be said to be literally fulfilled in this movement.[76]

Perhaps Anderson's strongest arguments in support of the Dispersion Theory were those which are still used by some Latter-day Saints today, and which first appeared in a letter by him dated January 29, 1927. In this letter, and through later books and writings, Anderson asked 43 questions, which questions were so well written that they immediately placed his opponents on the defensive, particularly those members of the Church who at that time still believed in the North Pole Theory and who were not well versed in the gospel and/or the most "commonly accepted meaning" of various scriptures. Anyone interested in further studying the Dispersion Theory should read all of Anderson's letter.[77] However, because three of Anderson's questions still come up today, this author has listed and briefly commented on them:

5. Why do some people say the Ten Tribes will come and "bring their records with them?" I have heard that preached thousands of times, but have never found a man who could produce

---

76. Charles W. Penrose, "Something About the Lost Tribes," *The Improvement Era*, October, 1910, pp. 1087-1088.

77. James H. Anderson, *The Present Time & Prophecy*, Deseret News Press, Salt Lake City, Utah, 1933, pp.145-149. Walt Whipple, *op. cit.*, pp. 23-24.

that statement authoritatively or anything like it. Where is it recorded?

14. Who is the prophet to lead "the Ten Tribes from the land of the north?" Does not the *Doctrine and Covenants*, 110:11, say it is Joseph Smith, to whom was given the keys of that leading?

32. Who said the "mountains of ice" should be melted by the Ten Tribes, instead of by the Lord's power, when the mountains shall flow down at His presence?[78]

In regards to question number five, this author would like to refer the reader to 2 Nephi 29:11-14, and 3 Nephi 16:4, which mentions that the Lord instructed "the other tribes of the house of Israel, which" He "has led away" to "write the words" which He spake "unto them." Therefore, it appears to this author, that if the Lost Ten Tribes were and are keeping records as the Lord has instructed them, that they would most likely bring such records with them. This viewpoint is maintained by the General Authorities and has been preached and written down on several occasions:

In the October Conference of 1916, Elder James E. Talmage stated that when "the tribes shall come . . . they shall be brought forth as hath been predicted; and *I say unto you there are those now living—aye, some here present—who shall live to read the records of the Lost Tribes of Israel . . . .*"

It was claimed as early as 1845, that the records of these people were to be revealed at the same time as the "returning of the Ten Tribes from the north country." This inference was made by the Twelve Apostles at this time in a proclamation to all the world. . . .

Wilford Woodruff, in 1880, said that ". . . their records and other choice treasures they will bring with them to Zion. These things are as true as God lives." . . . And Elder Charles W. Penrose has stated that the Lost Ten Tribes will bring their records with them when they return.[79]

---

78. *Ibid.*

79. Walt Whipple. *op. cit.*, pp. 23-24. *Note:* For additional references see: Orson Pratt, *Millennial Star*, March 1867, and the *Liahona* Vol. 3, p. 65. James E. Talmage, *The Articles of Faith*, 1917 edition, p. 340; 1924 edition. p. 513. Parley P. Pratt, *Journal of Discourses*, August 26, 1865. Vol. 3, pp. 185-186. Wilford Woodruff, *Journal History*, February 25, 1855. p. 4.

Concerning Anderson's questions numbers 14 and 32, Walt Whipple has accurately recognized:

> [These questions] are merely challenges of other theorists' interpretations. Of course these challenges are necessary primarily to tear down the so-called "traditions" of the north pole theory in order to establish the idea that they were totally dispersed throughout Europe.[80]

Nine years after the publication of Anderson's book *God's Covenant Race,* another writer, Earnest L. Whitehead, authored in 1947 a book entitled The House of Israel, A Treatise on the Destiny, History, and Identification of Israel in all the Five Branches.

In many ways Whitehead's book was quite similar to Anderson's book, in that he personally interpreted numerous scriptures, and upheld the main premise of the Dispersion Theory, "that the Lost Ten Tribes were totally scattered among the present nations of the earth . . . and were only lost as to their identity."[81] However, Whitehead added some new ideas and interpretations of his own to the Dispersion Theory: for he interpreted the parable on the "branches of Israel" in Jacob 5:1-77 (in the Book of Mormon) as meaning there were "four branches of Israel plus the main trunk." This, then, made a total of five locations on the earth, he said, which contained the blood of Israel. The major portion of his book is centered around these following five groups: (1) Jerusalem, (2) America (the Nephites), (3) Britain, (4) Scandinavia, and (5) Tahiti.[82] In his searches he felt that he had found evidence to indicate that Christ visited the latter three as he had promised in 3 Nephi 16:1, where he spoke of "other sheep." In addition, one of the evidences which he claims against the "north pole theory" is the prophecy contained in Jeremiah 3:18 (in the Bible), which states that the house of Judah and the house of Israel "shall come together out of the land of the north . . . . ," of which he said the arctic regions could not be a suitable abode for such a "chosen" people:[83]

> It will be of considerable surprise to some to know that the Lord did not intend to isolate His chosen vine in a part of the world where they would grow up completely isolated from other nations, or of the rest of the House of Israel. This is the fallacy

---

80. *Ibid.*

81. Earnest L Whitehead, *op cit.,* pp. 88-94. James H. Anderson, *The Present Time & Prophecy . . .., op. cit.,* p. 128.

82. Earnest L. Whitehead. *op cit.,* pp. 88-94. Walt Whipple, *op. cit.,* pp. 24-25.

83. *Ibid.*

of belief behind the "north-pole theory" which has existed for a century within the Church.[84]

Following the publication of Anderson's and Whitehead's books, the Dispersion Theory quickly grew in popularity among many Latter-day Saints.[85] Some apparently accepted it because it sounded "logical," while others felt "it revealed that the location of the Lost Ten Tribes was not a mystery," and that it "made sense for the Church to push so hard in their missionary effort."[86] Whatever the reason for its wide acceptance, it appears that by the late 1950's, the Dispersion Theory may have been accepted by as many as two out of every three members of the Church who expressed themselves as having a definite opinion as to where the Lost Ten Tribes might be."[87]

However, beginning in the 1960's, the Dispersion Theory apparently began losing its influence among the general membership of the Church.[88] Perhaps one of the reasons may have been the publication in 1962 of *Prophecy—Key to the Future,* by Duane S. Crowther, a well known LDS author and publisher. In his book, Crowther emphasized that the "Lost Ten Tribes" would "be revealed in the North Country" and later "'come to the New Jerusalem (America)." Although Crowther never specifically endorsed or criticized the validity of any of the previously mentioned four general theories—as to the possible whereabouts of the Lost Ten Tribes— he nevertheless wrote in such a literary manner as to suggest that their present *location* was still a "mystery," and thereby may have introduced some "caution" among many Latter-day Saints as to the particular validity of the Dispersion Theory.[89]

Then in 1971, Gerald N. Lund, another LDS author, wrote the book *The Coming of the Lord,* in which he went further than Crowther in pointing out that the Lost Ten Tribes "shall come as a body. . . ." His statement, quoted below, bluntly attacked the Dispersion Theory, and for that matter all the other three theories, by reminding the reader that all such "theories" were "only specu-

84. Earnest L. Whitehead, *op. cit.,* p. 85.

85. Walt Whipple, *op. cit.,* pp. 26-28. R. Clayton Brough, "Results of a Survey . . . ," *op. cit.*

86. R. Clayton Brough, "Results of a Survey . . ." *op. cit.*

87. Walt Whipple, *op. cit.,* pp. 26-28.

88. R. Clayton Brough, Results of a Survey . . ." *op, cit.*

89. Duane S. Crowther, *Prophecy, Key to the Future,* Bookcraft, Salt Lake City, Utah, 1962, pp. 117-126.

lation," since the "specific location" of the Lost Tribes "has not been revealed to the Church" (i.e.: it's still a mystery!):

Down through the centuries there have been innumerable speculations as to where the lost ten tribes are. These speculations have ranged all the way from a planet somewhere in outer space to exotic hidden places under the ice cap of the Arctic regions. Some have speculated that they went into present-day Europe, and became the various present nations of that continent. Some Church members seek to support this latter idea with the fact that many patriarchal blessings state that an individual is of the tribe of Ephraim (one of those lost), and also because of the great gathering of converts that has taken place since the early history of the Church out of the nations of Europe. (Since Europe is north of Palestine and Assyria in latitude, they feel this geographical location qualifies in the sense of being gathered from the lands of the north.)

All such speculation as to the whereabouts of this group of Israelites is strictly that—only speculation. As yet, their specific location has not been revealed to the Church. But the idea that the gathering has already been fulfilled in the great missionary efforts of the Church is in error, for the prophets have definitely stated that they shall come as a body; their coming shall be so miraculous that it could not be mistaken for a gradual response to missionary work.[90]

Both Crowther's and Lund's books were very well accepted by the general church membership when they were first introduced to

90. Gerald N. Lund, *The Coming of the Lord,* Bookcraft, Salt Lake City, Utah, 1971, pp. 160-161. *Note:* In reference to the Lost Ten Tribes and related individual lineages identified in Latter-day Saint patriarchal blessings." the following information is given: On February 17, 1978, this author wrote a letter to the Church Historian requesting statistical information on the number of patriarchal blessings which had been given to members of the Church that had been tabulated according to lineage identity. On March 7, 1978, he received a response from the Public Services division of the Church that such information, being of a sacred nature, was not available to the public. However, earlier, on August 17. 1977, this author had a telephone conversation with Church Patriarch Eldred G. Smith, during which Patriarch Smith mentioned that the number of patriarchal blessings which identified members of the Church as being from some other lineage than Ephraim, Manesseh. or Judah, were "very few in number," and in no way numbered enough to encourage belief in the theory that the Lost Ten Tribes of Israel had been entirely dispersed throughout the nations of the earth. Patriarch Smith additionally stated to this author that the 'Lost Ten Tribes are definitely still lost."

the Latter-day Saint public, and are still on the market today. As to whether they substantially contributed to the present decline in the acceptance of the Dispersion Theory among Latter-day Saints, can be debated. However, this author is inclined to believe they have; for although the Dispersion Theory still seems to be the most widely accepted theory of any of the four major theories discussed herein, Latter-day Saints appear to now accept it with only a possible margin of five out of every nine persons, rather than the possible two out of every three persons of nearly two decades ago.[91] And, considering that General Authorities of the Church have consistently taught that "at least a sufficient number or large portion of the Lost Ten Tribes are still united today as one body or group of people, who sometime in these Last Days shall return from the land of the north," it is perhaps best that the Dispersion Theory is being viewed today with much greater caution.

Since the first edition of this book was published, there have been several articles and books written by Latter-day Saints which have discussed the possible "present whereabouts" of the Lost Ten Tribes of Israel. For example:

> Where [the Lost Ten Tribes] went is not known, and this fact has led to much speculation about their present whereabouts. The Lord has not seen fit to reveal their location, however, and until he does so, it is useless to try to identify their present locality. (*Old Testament: 1 Kings-Malachi*; Religion 302, Student Manual, LDS Church, 1982, p.115.)

Vern G . Swanson, "Israel's Other Tribes" *The Ensign*, LDS Church, January, 1982, p. 31:

> Certainly all the reasons why the Lord "hid" the tribes—as he did with both Ephriam and Manasseh—and exactly when we will identify the others and when a distinct remnant of "they who are in the north countries" will come to "the boundaries of the everlasting hills" is information that remains with God.

Bruce R. McConkie, *The Millennial Messiah: The Second Coming of the Son of Man*, Deseret Book,1982, p. 320:

> These Ten Tribes, no matter where they are located, are in nations and places known in the days of Isaiah and Jeremiah and the ancient prophets as the north countries.

---

91. Walt Whipple, *op. cit.*, 26-28. R. Clayton Brough, "Results of a Survey . . . ," *op. cit..* See page 42, footnote number 5.

Bruce R. McConkie, *A New Witness For The Articles of Faith,*
Deseret Book, 1985, p. 520:

> There is something mysterious and fascinating about
> believing the Ten Tribes are behind an iceberg somewhere in the
> land of the north, or that they are on some distant planet that
> will one day join itself with the earth or that the tribe of Dan is
> in Denmark, the tribe of Reuben in Russia, and so forth. A com-
> mon cliche asserts: "If we knew where the Lost Tribes were, they
> would not be lost." True it is that they are lost from the knowl-
> edge of the world; they are not seen and recognized as the king-
> dom they once were; but in general terms, their whereabouts is
> known. They are scattered in all nations of the earth, primarily
> in the nations north of the lands of their first inheritance.

Additional comments and opinions by Elder McConkie on
the "return" and "restoration" of the Lost Ten Tribes can be
found in *The Millennial Messiah: The Second Coming of the Son
of Man,* Deseret Book, 1982, pp. 319-329, and *A New Witness
For The Articles of Faith*, Deseret Book, 1985, pp. 520-521,
529-530, 641-642.

Summary

   As was presented in Chapter Two of this book, the General
Authorities of the Church have consistently taught that even
though "some of the backsliding Israelites rebelled and turned
aside from the main body of the Lost Ten Tribes as it traveled northward," thereby "becoming the leaven to leaven with the promised
seed all the nations of the earth," nevertheless, "at least a sufficient
number or large portion of the Lost Ten Tribes are still united today
as one body or group of people, who sometime in these Last Days
shall return from the land of the north."[92]

   However, as indicated in this chapter, just where this "sufficient
number or large portion" of people of the Lost Ten Tribes are now
located has not yet been revealed by the Lord, although there have
been various speculations and theories advanced by leaders and
members of the Church alike as to their possible present location.

   In regards to the four theories mentioned in this chapter, or any
others for that matter, this writer would like to suggest that it would
be wise for all of us, particularly as Latter-day Saints, to not place

92. See Chapter Two in this book.

our "faith" in "theories and/or speculations," for we have been cautioned by our General Authorities that we have no knowledge of the location of "that part of the Ten Tribes who went into the north country."[93]

In conclusion, we may rest assured that the first people on earth to whom the location of the Lost Ten Tribes will be revealed, will be to "the prophets and chosen Saints of God. They will know the exact location and whereabouts of the lost tribes long before any scientists or society will discover it;"[94] for "Surely the Lord God will do nothing but he revealeth his secret unto his servants the prophets" (Amos 3:7)

Therefore, may we all strive as Latter-day Saints to learn that which has already been given to us, while diligently preparing ourselves to receive that which has yet to be revealed.

---

93. Franklin D. Richards and James A. Little, *A Compendium of the Doctrines of the Gospel.* Deseret News, Salt Lake City, Utah, 1914, p. 88. Bruce R McConkie. *op. cit.*, p. 455. See also Chapters 2 and 3 of this book.

94. W. Cleon Skousen, *Prophecy & Modern Times,* Deseret Book Company, Salt Lake City, Utah, 1950, pp. 55-56.

Four

Prophecies: The Return Of The Lost Tribes

Events of the Last Days Which Will Precede the Return of the Lost Tribes

The return in the last days of the Lost Ten Tribes of Israel has been the subject of many of the discourses given by General Authorities of the Church. Indeed, the insight, comprehension, and commentaries by the Brethren of the Church on the various scriptural passages relating to the Last Days, and particularly to the return of the Lost Ten Tribes from the "land of the north," has received such attention throughout the history of the Church that today their comments relative to the return of the Lost Ten Tribes are found in numerous Latter-day Saint books, magazines, and other writings.

To begin with, the General Authorities of the Church have repeatedly taught that certain events will proceed the eventual and miraculous "return of the Lost Ten Tribes from the land of the north."[1] The first of these events will apparently be the "fulfilling of the times of the Gentiles," of which Elder Orson Pratt has stated:

> The great object of the angel in restoring the Gospel was, in the first place, to fulfill the times of the Gentiles. Inquires one— "What do you mean by that?" I mean that God will send this Gospel, restored by an angel, to every nation, kindred, people, and tongue in the Gentile world before he will permit his servants to go to the scattered remnants of Israel.[2]

1. Duane S. Crowther, *op. cit..* pp. 19-21, 32, 117-11. & Bruce R. McConkie, *op. cit.,* pp. 715-734.
2. Orson Pratt, *Journal of Discourses,* Vol. 18, pp. 176-177. March 26, 1876.

The restoration of the gospel and taking of that gospel to the Gentile nations marked the beginning, or ushering in, of the times of the Gentiles. A future turning away from the Gentiles, when they will cease to be receptive to the missionary message, will mark the fulfilling of the times of the Gentiles, while at the same time initiating a major effort to preach the gospel to the House of Israel.

Elder Pratt further stated that not only would "the times of the Gentiles" be "fulfilled" prior to the return of the Lost Ten Tribes, but also that the time would come when we, as a Church, instead of trying to convert the Gentile nations of the world, would instruct our missionaries to "go unto the remnants of the house of Israel that are scattered in the four quarters of the earth:"

> Go unto the remnants of the house of Israel that are scattered in the four quarters of the earth. Go and proclaim to them that the times of their dispersion are accomplished; that the times of the Gentiles are fulfilled; that the time has arrived for my people Israel, who have been scattered for generations in a dark and cloudy day, to gather unto their own homes again, and to build up old Jerusalem on its former heap. And then will commence the gathering of the Jews to old Jerusalem; then the ten tribes in the northern regions, wherever they may be, after having been concealed from the nations for twenty-five hundred years, will come forth and will return.[3]

At this point, it is interesting to note that the present gathering of the Jewish people back to their homeland of Palestine is now only a "preparatory gathering," and that a larger and more complete gathering is yet in the future—after the "times of the Gentiles" have been "fulfilled," and the Lost Ten Tribes come to "Zion" (on the American continent). For on March 7, 1831, the Lord revealed to the Prophet Joseph Smith that the Jews would be "gathered again," but not until the "times of the Gentiles be fulfilled" (D&C 45:25). In addition, the Lord revealed in the Book of Mormon (3 Nephi 21) that the main gathering of the Jews to Palestine was to take place after the building of the New Jerusalem and the coming of the Ten Tribes to Zion; at which time

> . . . shall the work commence, with the Father, among all nations; in preparing the way whereby his people may be gathered home to the land of their inheritance.

---

3 Orson Pratt, Ibid., Vol. 18, p. 64, July 25, 1875.

And they shall go out from all nations; and they shall not go
out in haste, nor go by flight, for I will go before them, saith the
Father, and I will be their rearward (3 Nephi 21:28-29).[4]

Between the period of time when the "times of the Gentiles are
fulfilled" and the Lost Ten Tribes return from the "land of the
north," there are two other events which must also take place: one
is the building of the "New Jerusalem" or the "City of Zion" in
Jackson County, Missouri. The other is the "Cleansing of the earth
of much of its iniquity."

Concerning the building of the city of the "New Jerusalem" in
Jackson County, Missouri, prior to the return of the Lost Ten
Tribes from the "land of the north," Elder Orson Pratt has stated:

After Zion is built in Jackson County, and after the Temple
is built upon that spot of ground where the corner stone was laid
in 1831; after the glory of God in the form of a cloud by day shall
rest upon that Temple, and by night the shining of a flaming fire
will fill the whole heavens round about; after every dwelling
place upon Mount Zion shall be clothed upon as with a pillar of
fire by night, and a cloud by day, about that period of time, the
ten tribes will be heard of, away in the north, a great company,
as Jeremiah says, coming down from the northern regions, coming to sing in the height of the latter-day Zion.[5]

And Duane S. Crowther has written:

It appears that the long anticipated coming of the Ten
Tribes from the north will take place shortly after or possibly just
before Zion has been sanctified and the Lord has come to the
temple. Oliver Cowdery stated that the Angel Moroni instructed
Joseph Smith that after the Church "shall be sanctified and
receive an inheritance where the glory of God shall rest upon
them . . . and all things are prepared, the ten tribes of Israel will
be revealed in the north country, whither they have been for a
long season."

It should be recalled also that the order shown in 3 Nephi
21:22-26 . . . showed that first the building of the New Jerusalem would have begun. then the Lamanites would be gathered

---

4. Duane S. Crowther, *op. cit.*, pp. 127-128. For other references and
expanded information regarding the return of the Jewish people to Palestine in
the Last Days, see: Duane S. Crowther, *Prophecy—Key to The Future*, Horizon
Publishers. (See Selected Bibliography in this book.)

5. Orson Pratt, *Journal of Discourses*, Vol. 18, p. 68. July 25, 1875.

in, then the Savior would appear and "at that day shall the work of the Father commence among all the dispersed of my people, yea, even the tribes which have been lost." (3 Nephi 21:26)[6]

Regarding the "cleansing of the earth of much of its iniquity" prior to the return of the Lost Ten Tribes from the "north country," the Prophet Joseph Smith has stated that:

Pestilence, hail, famine, and earthquake will sweep the wicked of this generation from off the face of the land, to open and prepare the way for the return of the lost tribes of Israel from the north country.[7]

And President Joseph Fielding Smith has likewise said:

We discover from the declaration by the Prophet to the people of the world, that the cleansing of the earth of much of its iniquity, by blood, fire, earthquake, pestilence and the display of angry elements, was to assist in preparing the way for the return of the lost tribes of Israel. We should not be confused. The call for the gathering of scattered Israel had been proclaimed three years earlier and the missionaries had been hard at work gathering into the fold those of Israel who had scattered themselves among the Gentiles. The great day of the coming of the lost tribes would be after the preparatory work had been accomplished in the destruction of the wickedness in very great measure, and the way prepared in part for the coming of the Lord also and the building of his Holy City and Temple.[8]

In conclusion. in reference to the preceding remarks by Presidents Joseph Smith and Joseph Fielding Smith about the occurrences of earthquakes, Duane S. Crowther has commented that possibly the "great earthquake" mentioned in the Book of Revelation, may precede the return of the Lost Ten Tribes:[9]

---

6. Duane S. Crowther, *op. cit.*, p. 117.

7. Joseph Smith, *History of the Church*, Deseret Book Company. Salt Lake City, Utah, 1946-1951. Vol. 1, p. 315.

8. Joseph Fielding Smith, *Church History and Modern Revelation*, a Melchizedek Priesthood Course of Study Published by the Council of the Twelve Apostles of The Church of Jesus Christ of Latter-day Saints, Salt Lake Cily, Utah, 1948. Vol. 2, p. 141.

9. Duane S. Crowther. *op. cit.*, p. 118.

And I beheld when he had opened the sixth seal, and lo, there was a great earthquake; and the sun became black as sackcloth of hair, and the moon became as blood;

And the stars of heaven fell unto the earth, even as a fig tree casteth her untimely figs, when she is shaken of a mighty wind.

And the heaven departed as a scroll when it is rolled together; and every mountain and island were moved out of their places. (Revelation 6:12-14)

The Coming of the Lost Ten Tribes from the Land of the North

Following the period when the "times of the Gentiles is fulfilled" and Zion [an area encompassing the city of the New Jerusalem] "is built in Jackson County and . . . the Temple is built upon that spot of ground where the corner stone was laid in 1831," and after the "cleansing of the earth of much of its iniquity, by blood, fire, earthquake, pestilence and the display of angry elements," then, as Elder Orson Pratt has stated: "the ten tribes will be heard of, away in the north, a great company, as Jeremiah says, coming down from the northern regions, coming to sing in the height of the Latter-day Zion."[10]

Indeed, the return of the "great company" of the Lost Ten Tribes from the "land of the north," will be one of the most miraculous events which will take place in the last days, prior to the Battle of Armageddon and the appearance of the Lord Jesus Christ on the Mount of Olives in Jerusalem.[11] In reference to the specific events which will transpire when the Lost Ten Tribes return from the "north countries," the 133rd section of the Doctrine and Covenants contains the following prophecy:

And they who are in the north countries shall come in remembrance before the Lord; and *their prophets shall hear his voice, and shall no longer stay themselves; and they shall smite the rocks, and the ice shall flow down at their presence.*

And an *highway shall be cast up in the midst of the great deep. Their enemies shall become a prey unto them,*

---

10. Orson Pratt. *Journal of Discourses*, Vol. 18, p. 68, July 25, 1875. Duane S. Crowther, *op. cit.*, p. 182.

11. Duane S Crowther, *op. cit.*, Inside Jacket Diagram. Orson Pratt, *Journal of Discourses*, Vol. 18, p. 68, July 25, 1875. *Note:* For more details on other events of the Last Days. read: Duane S Crowther, *Prophecy—Key to the Future;* Joseph Fielding Smith, *Signs of the Times;* Gerald N. Lund, *The Coming of the Lord.* See the Selected Bibliography in this book.)

And in the barren deserts there shall come forth pools of living water; and the parched ground shall no longer be a thirsty land.

And they shall bring forth their rich treasures unto the children of Ephraim, my servants.

And the boundaries of the everlasting hills shall tremble at their presence.

And there shall they fall down and be crowned with glory, even in Zion, by the hands of the servants of the Lord, even the children of Ephraim.

And they shall be filled with songs of everlasting joy.

Behold, this is the blessing of the everlasting God upon the tribes of Israel, and the richer blessing upon the head of Ephraim and his fellows.[12]

It appears from this prophecy that the coming of the Lost Ten Tribes from the "north countries" will not be without incident, for those people then comprising the Lost Ten Tribes will have to deal with their enemies during their advance, and the boundaries or entire land of the everlasting hills (a term used to identify the American continents) will shake and tremble as they come to Zion.

Commenting on this prophetic scripture, Elder Orson Pratt has stated:

Some forty-three years ago, in speaking of the lost ten tribes of Israel, the Lord says—"They who are in the north countries shall come in remembrance before the Lord, and their Prophets shall hear his voice, and shall no longer stay themselves; and they shall smite the rocks, and the ice shall flow down at their presence. And an highway shall be cast up in the midst of the great deep. Their enemies shall become a prey unto them, and in the barren deserts there shall come forth pools of living water; and the parched ground shall no longer be a thirsty land. And they shall bring forth their rich treasures unto the children of Ephraim my servants. And the boundaries of the everlasting hills shall tremble "at their presence." To show that they come with power, they come on a highway cast up for them; the ice feels the power of God and flows down, making room for them; and the barren deserts of the north, wherever they may go and need water, will yield forth pools of living water to quench their thirst. As they come to sing in the height of Zion, the everlasting hills, this great Rocky Mountain range, extending from the

_____
12. Doctrine and Covenants 133:26-34; italics added.

arctic regions south to the central portions of America, will tremble beneath the power of God at the approach of that people.
Then will be fulfilled the saying of David, that the mountains
shall skip like rams, and the little hills like lambs, before his people. The very trees of the field will clap like hands, as the
Psalmist David has said. Then will be fulfilled the passage that
was quoted yesterday by brother Woodruff—"Sing O heavens, be
joyful O earth, and break forth into singing O mountains, for the
Lord hath redeemed his people," &c. And when they get to Zion
they will begin to say—"The place is too strait for me, give place
to me that I may dwell;" then the saying will go forth—"Behold I
was a captive. Zion was a captive, moving to and fro, tossed to
and fro, and not comforted. Behold I was left alone." But where
have this great company been, where has this mighty host come
from? They have come from their hiding place in the north country; they have been led thence by the Prophets of the Most High
God, the Lord going before their camp, talking with them out of
the cloud, as he talked in ancient days with the camp of Israel,
uttering his voice before his army, for his camp will be very great.
So says the Prophet Joel, and his prophecy will be fulfilled.
When they return to Zion to sing in the height thereof, "They will
fall down there and be crowned with glory by the hands of the
servants of the Lord, even the children of Ephraim."[13]

In addition, Elder Pratt has also inferred that the Lost Ten Tribes
will return from the land of the north "after the six thousand years
have ended . . . probably . . . in the morning of the seventh thousand years" and will "come to this land, to be crowned with glory in
the midst of the City of "Zion":

> Then again, after the six thousand years have ended, before
> the Lord shall come while these trumpets are sounding, or
> about that time, we find that there is to be a great work among
> the nations—which will probably take place in the morning of
> the seventh thousand years. The ten tribes will have to come
> forth and come to this land, to be crowned with glory in the
> midst of Zion by the hands of the servants of God, even the
> Children of Ephraim.[14] [See also pp. 103-104 in this book.]

---

13. Orson Pratt, *Journal of Discourses*, Vol. 18, p. 24, April 11, 1875.
14. Orson Pratt, *Journal of Discourses*, Vol. 16, p. 325, November 22, 1873.

Similar to the prior statements of Elder Pratt, President Wilford Woodruff has likewise said:

The ten tribes of Israel in the north country will come in remembrance before God in due time, and they will smite the rocks and the mountains of ice will flow down before them, and the everlasting hills will tremble at their presence. A highway will be cast up through the midst of the great deep for them to come to Zion.[15]

Also Brother W. Cleon Skousen has written:

Regardless of where the Ten Tribes are, it will require a miracle to bring them forth. It will be of greater magnitude than the dividing of the Red Sea in the days of Israel's Exodus. The day is coming when the seed of Jacob will no longer say, "The Lord liveth that brought up the Children of Israel out of the land of Egypt; but the Lord liveth that brought up the Children of Israel out of the North" (Jeremiah 16:14-15)

Mountains, ice and a continent of water will stand between the Ten Tribes and the land of Zion when they first appear, but they will "smite the rocks, and the ice shall flow down at their presence" (D&C 133:26). As they come to the great body of water, dry land will be cast up in the midst of it so that a mighty highway will spread before them. (D&C 133:27; Isa. 11:16) Thus will the God of Jacob fulfill his promise to bring them back to the land of Joseph and crown them with mighty blessings under the hands of the Ephraimite Saints. (D&C 133:32)

Where will the hosts of Israel dwell?

It has been previously pointed out that if the great gentile civilization now inhabiting this land should become unworthy of it, the Lord has warned that he will rid the land of them. Joseph Smith predicted that there would be ample room for the hosts of Israel when they come. He said that the judgments of the Lord "will sweep the wicked of this generation from off the face of the land, to open and prepare the way for the return of the lost tribes of Israel from the north country." (*Teachings of the Prophet Joseph Smith*, p. 17) It is apparent that this prophecy is yet to be fulfilled.

It would appear that some of the gentiles who are driven by war and pestilence will seek respite in the northern portion of the continent where they can continue their lives after the

15. Wilford Woodruff, *Journal of Discourses*, Vol. 18, p. 127, October 8, 1875.

design of their own wickedness. Such a people would no doubt
resist the migration of the multitudes of Israel as they pour
across the great highway. The scriptures plainly speak of the
Ten Tribes being confronted by "enemies" who will become their
"prey" as they march over them on the way to the capital city of
the New Jerusalem. (D&C 133:28)

And any people, not of Israel, who think they can avail
themselves of the great highway and thus flee into the former
habitation of the Ten Tribes will be as surprised and disap-
pointed as the armies of Egypt who attempt to cross dry-shod
on the miraculous thoroughfare that opened up suddenly in the
midst of the Red Sea. The mighty highway of the latter day will
be equally unsafe for the wicked who trespass on it, for Israel
alone shall pass over it. (Isaiah 35:8-10)[16]

As the Lost Ten Tribes return from the "land of the north" or the
"north countries," and "come to this land [of America], to be
crowned with glory in the midst of "Zion,"[17] their "leading . . . from
the land of the north" will take place under the "direction of the
President of The Church of Jesus Christ of Latter-day Saints.
Regarding this matter, Elder Bruce R. McConkie has written:

In due course the Lost Tribes of Israel will return and come
to the children of Ephraim to receive their blessings. This great
gathering will take place under the direction of the President of
The Church of Jesus Christ of Latter-day Saints, for he holds the
keys of "the gathering of Israel from the four parts of the earth,
and the leading of the ten tribes from the land of the north."
(D&C 110:11) Keys are the right of presidency, the power to
direct; and by this power the Lost Tribes will return. . . .[18]

When in the Last Days the Ten tribes return from the "land of
the north," they will no longer be lost. They will become recognized
for whom they are, and for the importance of what they shall bring.
As Elder McConkie has additionally stated, The Ten Tribes "will
return with 'their prophets' and their scriptures to be 'crowned with
glory, even in Zion, by the hands of the servants of the Lord, even

---

16. W. Cleon Skousen, *Prophecy & Modern Times, op. cit.,* pp. 56-58. *Note:*
In Isaiah 54:2-3, and 3 Nephi 21-26; 22:3, it is inferred that when the Ten
Tribes come to the area of the New Jersualem, they will inhabit the nearby
desolate cities of the Gentiles.

17. Orson Pratt, *Journal of Discourses,* Vol. 16, p. 325, November 22, 1873.

18. Bruce R. McConkie, *op. cit.,* p. 458.

the children of Ephraim.'"[19] Concerning the "prophets" who will then be with the Ten Tribes, and the "scriptural records" which the Ten Tribes shall bring with them when they come to the New Jerusalem, Elder Orson Pratt has stated:

Having spoken concerning the gathering of the ten tribes, I will refer again to their Prophets. "Their Prophets shall hear his voice. Do not think that we are the only people who will have Prophets. God is determined to raise up Prophets among that people, but he will not bestow upon them all the fulness of the blessings of the Priesthood. The fulness will be reserved to be given to them after they come to Zion. But Prophets will be among them while in the north, and a portion of the Priesthood will be there; and John the Revelator will be there, teaching, instructing and preparing them for this great work; for to him were given the keys for the gathering of Israel, at the time when he wrote that little book while on the Isle of Patmos. At that time, John was a very old man; but the Lord told him that he must yet prophesy before many kingdoms, and nations, and peoples, and tongues, and he has got that mission to perform, and in the last days the spirit and power of Elias will attend his adminis- trations among these ten tribes, and he will assist in preparing them to return to this land. . . .[20]

And also:

The Book of Mormon informs us that the ten tribes in the north country will have a record as well as the Jews, a Bible of their own, if you please. Indeed Jesus after having instructed the remnant of Joseph upon this land and revealed to them His gospel, said to them, "But now I go unto the Father, and also to show myself unto the lost tribes of Israel, for they are not lost unto the Father, for He knoweth whither He hath taken them." And it was predicted concerning them by one of the ancient American prophets, who lived in those days, that when God should bring these ten tribes from the north country, they would bring their records with them. And it should come to pass that they should have the records of the Nephites, and the Nephites should have the records of the Jews, and the Jews and the Nephites should have the records of the lost tribes of the house of Israel, and the lost tribes of Israel should have the records of the Nephites and the Jews. "It shall come to pass that I will gather

---

19. *Ibid.*
20. Orson Pratt, *Journal of Discourses*, Vol. 18, pp. 25-26, April 11, 1875.

my people together, and I will also gather my word in one." Not only the people are to be gathered from the distant portions of our globe, but their records, or bibles, will also be united in one. [See 2 Nephi:29:12-14][21]

Elder James E. Talmage expressed in the Church Conferences of 1916 his belief that "some" of the Latter-day Saints then attending the October Conference of that year would "live to read the records of the Lost Tribes of Israel":

There is a tendency among men to explain away what they don't wish to understand in literal simplicity, and we, as Latter-day Saints are not entirely free from the taint of that tendency. . . Some people say that prediction is to be explained in this way: A gathering is in progress, and has been in progress from the early days of this Church; and thus the "Lost Tribes" are now being gathered; but that we are not to look for the return of any body of people now unknown as to their whereabouts. True, the gathering is in progress, this is a gathering dispensation; *but the prophecy stands that the tribes shall be brought forth from their hiding place bringing their scriptures with them, which scriptures shall become one with the scriptures of the Jews, the holy Bible, and with the scriptures of the Nephites, the Book of Mormon, and with the scriptures of the Latter-day Saints as embodied in the volumes of modern revelation. . . .*[22]

The tribes shall come; they are not lost unto the Lord; they shall be brought forth as hath been predicted; *and I say unto you, there are those now living—aye, some here present—who shall live to read the records of the Lost Tribes of Israel,* which shall be made one with the record of the Jews, or the Holy Bible, and the record of the Nephites, or the Book of Mormon, even as the Lord hath predicted.[23]

When the Ten Tribes "come to the height of Zion" in the Last Days, Elder Orson Pratt has said that "they shall be crowned with glory under the hands of the servants of God living in those days." In other words, they will be "crowned with certain blessings that pertain to the Priesthood that they could not receive in their own lands."[24] President Wilford Woodruff has explained what this "crowning of certain blessings" will consist of:

21. Orson Pratt, *Journal of Discourses,* Vol. 19, p.172, December 2, 1877.
22. James E. Talmage, *Conference Report,* April, 1916, p. 130. (Italics added.)
23. *Ibid.,* October 1916, p. 76. (Italics added.)

Again, here are the ten tribes of Israel, we know nothing about them only what the Lord has said by His Prophets. There are Prophets among them, and by and by they will come along, and they will smite the rocks, and the mountains of ice will flow down at their presence, and a highway will be cast up before them, and *they will come to Zion, receive their endowments, and be crowned under the hands of the children of Ephraim, and there are persons before me in this assembly today, who will assist to give them their endowments.*[25]

Latter-day Saints have often wondered how long the Ten Tribes will "tarry in the heights of Zion" after they come from the "land of the north." Concerning this matter, Elder Orson Pratt has expressed:

How long will they who come from the north countries tarry in the heights of Zion? Sometime. They have got to raise wheat, cultivate the grape, wine and oil, raise flocks and herds, and their souls will have to become as a watered garden. They will dwell in Zion a good while.[26]

Regarding the responsible activities which the Ten Tribes will become involved in during the time they "dwell in Zion a good while," Elder Pratt has concluded that "twelve thousand [High Priests] out of each of these ten tribes . . . [will] go forth to all people, nations, kindreds, and tongues, for the salvation of the remnants of Israel in the four quarters of the earth, to bring as many as will come unto the Church . . . . and when they have completed His work here on the earth, they will be called home to Zion . . ." :

The ten tribes will believe in Christ, so much so, that he will lead them, while on their return from the north country, and they will come and "sing in the height of Zion," and they will not sorrow any more at all:" whereas the Jews will have no such favours shown unto them on their return from the nations, but will have great distress and sorrow, and mourning, after they get back to Jerusalem. The ten tribes are redeemed from their afflictions before the Jews, consequently they first come to Zion

---

24. Orson Pratt, *Journal of Discourses*, Vol. 18, p. 69, July 25, 1875. *Note:* Saints now in the spirit World could assist in the endowment work of the Lost Ten Tribes.

25. Wilford Woodruff, *Journal of Discourses*, Vol. 4, pp. 231-232, February 22, 1857.

26. Orson Pratt, *Journal of Discourses*, Vol. 18, p. 25, April 11, 1875.

among the redeemed saints, and partake with them in all the glory of Zion. . [27]

In that day will be set apart twelve thousand out of each of these ten tribes, one hundred and twenty thousand persons ordained to the High Priesthood, after the order of the Son of God to go forth to all people, nations, kindreds and tongues, for the salvation of the remnants of Israel in the four quarters of the earth, to bring as many as will come unto the Church of the firstborn. . . .[28]

And twelve thousand High Priests will be elected from each of these ten tribes, as well as from the scattered tribes, and sealed in their foreheads, and will be ordained and receive power to gather out of all nations, kindreds, tongues and people as many as will come unto the general assemblage of the Church of the first-born. Will not that be a great work? Imagine one hundred and forty-four thousand High Priests going forth among the nations, and gathering out as many as will come to the Church of the first-born. All that will be done, probably, in the morning of the seventh thousand years. . . .[29]

Thus God will have twelve thousand out of all the tribes of Israel to fulfill his purposes; and when they have completed his work here on the earth, they will be called home to Zion, be crowned with glory and stand upon Mount Zion and sing the song of the redeemed, the song of the hundred and forty-four thousand, and the Father's name will be written in their fore-heads. . . .[30]

The Ten Tribes will Leave America and Return to Palestine

As Elder Orson Pratt has previously stated, the Ten Tribes of Israel will, in the Last Days, "dwell in Zion a good while," and from there many of them will "go forth to all people, nations. kindreds and tongues, for the salvation of the remnants of Israel in the four quarters of the earth, to bring as many as will come unto the Church." [31]

---

27. Orson Pratt. *Millennial Star,* Vol. 11, p. 323, November, 1849.
28. Orson Pratt. *Journal of Discourses,* Vol. 18, p. 68, July 25, 1875.
29. Orson Pratt. *Journal of Discourses,* Vol. 16, p. 325, November 22, 1873.
30. Orson Pratt. *Journal of Discourses,* Vol. 18, p. 68, July 25, 1875.
31. Orson Pratt. Journal of Discourses, Vol. 18, p. 25, April 11, 1875; Vol. 18, p. 68. July 25, 1875.

However, the Ten Tribes will not remain indefinitely in "Zion" (the area which includes the city of the New Jerusalem, in Jackson County, Missouri), for the Lord has prophesied, and promised that in the last days He would "remember" His "covenant" to His "people," and eventually bring the Twelve Tribes of "the house of Israel" back again to "Jerusalem"—the "land of their inheritance." (3 Nephi 20:21-36)[32]

Regarding this prophetic promise, Elder Orson Pratt, commenting on the following prophecy by Ezekiel, specifically wrote in 1849 that the Ten Tribes will "first come to Zion among the redeemed saints, and partake with them in all the glory of Zion, until the Jews and Jerusalem shall also be redeemed, [then] they [the Ten Tribes] shall return to Jerusalem, and receive their inheritance in the land of Palestine, according to the divisions of that land in Ezekiel's prophecy, and become one nation with the Jews, in the land upon the mountains of Israel."[33] Ezekiel's prophecy is as follows:

> . . . Thus saith the Lord God; Behold, I will take the children of Israel from among the heathen, whither they be gone, and will gather them on every side, and bring them into their own land:
>
> And I will make them one nation in the land upon the mountains of Israel; and one king shall be king to them all: and they shall be no more two nations, neither shall they be divided into two kingdoms any more at all. . . .
>
> And they shall dwell in the land that I have given unto Jacob my servant, wherein your fathers have dwelt; and they shall dwell therein, even they, and their children, and their children's children for ever. . . . (Ezekiel 37:21-22, 25)

In 1875, Elder Pratt additionally stated that "when the Jews have received their scourging, and Jesus has descended upon the Mount of Olives ['in the midst of the great battle of 'Armageddon'], [then] the ten tribes will leave Zion, and will go to Palestine, to inherit the land that was given to their ancient fathers. . . :"[34]

> By and by, when all things are prepared—when the Jews have received their scourging, and Jesus has descended upon the Mount of Olives, the ten tribes will leave Zion, and will go to Palestine, to inherit the land that was given to their ancient

32. Joseph Fielding Smith, *Doctrines of Salvation*, Vol. 2, pp. 248-250.

33. Orson Pratt, *Millennial Star*, Vol. 11, p. 323, November 1, 1849.

34. Orson Pratt, *Journal ot Discourses*, Vol. 7, pp. 188-190, July 10, 1859. Charles W. Penrose, *Millennial Star*, Vol. 21, p. 583, September 10, 1859.

fathers, and it will be divided amongst the descendants of Abraham, Isaac and Jacob by the inspiration of the Holy Ghost. They will go there to dwell in peace in their own land from that time, until the earth shall pass away. But Zion, after their departure, will still remain upon the western hemisphere, and she will be crowned with glory as well as old Jerusalem, and, as the Psalmist David says, she will become the joy of the whole earth. "Beautiful for situation is Mount Zion on the sides of the north, the city of the great King."[35]

Therefore, eventually in the last days the Ten Tribes of Israel will again return to the land of Palestine, from which they were led away nearly 2,700 years ago. Their initial coming as "a body of people" from "The land of the north to Zion," and their later return to the land of Palestine, will be two of the most significant events of the last days.

That we will all be found worthy and prepared when these and other prophecies come to pass, is this author's sincere hope and prayer; for as Elder Orson Pratt has so wisely stated: "Latter-day Saints should be wide awake, and should not have their minds engaged in . . . fooleries. . . . We should put these things away, and our inquiry should be—'Lord, how can we prepare the way before thy coming? . . . How can we be prepared to behold the Saints who lived on the earth in former dispensations . . . ?":

> After the six thousand years have ended, before the Lord shall come while these trumpets are sounding, or about that time, we find that there is to be a great work among the nations— which will probably take place in the morning of the seventh thousand years. The ten tribes will have to come forth and come to this land, to be crowned with glory in the midst of Zion by the hands of the servants of God, even the Children of Ephraim; and twelve thousand High Priests will be elected from each of these ten tribes, as well as from the scattered tribes, and sealed in their foreheads, and will be ordained and receive power to gather out of all nations, kindreds, tongues and people as many as will come unto the general assemblage of the Church of the first-born. Will not that be a great work? Imagine one hundred and forty-four thousand High Priests going forth among the nations, and gathering out as many as will come to the Church of the first-born. All that will be done, probably, in the morning

---

35. Orson Pratt, *Journal of Discourses*, Vol. 18, p. 68, July 25, 1875.

of the seventh thousand years. The work is of great magnitude, Latter-day Saints, and we are living almost upon the eve of it. Six thousand years have nearly gone by, the world is getting aged, and Satan has accomplished almost all that the Lord intends that he shall accomplish, before the day of rest. With a work of such magnitude before them, the Latter-day Saints should be wide awake, and should not have their minds engaged in those fooleries in which many indulge at the present time. We should put these things away, and our inquiry should be,—"Lord, how can we prepare the way before thy coming? How can we prepare ourselves to perform the great work which must be performed in this greatest of dispensations, the dispensation of the fullness of times? How can we be prepared to behold the Saints who lived on the earth in former dispensations, and take them by the hand and fall upon their necks and they fall upon ours, and we embrace each other? How can we be prepared for this?" How can all things that are in Christ Jesus, both which are in heaven and on earth, be assembled in one grand assembly, without we are wide awake?

May God bless you. Amen.[36]

36. Orson Pratt. *Journal of Discourses*, Vol. 16, pp. 325-326, November 22, 1873.

Appendix

(For numerical results of the survey below, see in this book: page 42, footnote 5.)
Survey Sheet

Latter day Saint Opinions on the Present Possible Whereabouts of the Lost Ten Tribes of Israel

Since the time of the Prophet Joseph Smith up to our own day, a number of General Authorities and members of the Church have often expressed their own beliefs and or opinions as to where the Lost Ten Tribes may be located at the present time. Through much research and a number of recent interviews, these theories have been classified under the following four categories:

1. **The Unknown Planet Theory**—(sometimes called incorrectly the "North Star Theory") which proposes that the Lost Ten Tribes were taken away from this earth in a manner similar to that of the City of Enoch, and that they now reside on another planet, orb, sphere, and/or near another star somewhere in the universe.

2. **The Hollow Earth (or Concave) Theory**—which proposes that the Lost Ten Tribes possibly reside in either an unknown concave area, like in a volcano, or in a great hollow area, somewhere in the region of the North Pole.

3. **The North Pole Theory**—which proposes that the Lost Ten Tribes possibly live in a mysteriously camouflaged area somewhere near or at the North Pole.

4. **The Dispersion Theory**—which proposes that the Lost Ten Tribes are today totally scattered among the present nations of the earth, and are only lost as to their identity—not as to their location—and are presently being gathered into the Church through missionary labors.

Request: To help in the determination of the attitudes of various members of the Church today on this subject, it would be appreciated if you have a specific opinion or belief regarding the present possible location of the Lost Ten Tribes if you would indicate which, if any, of the above theories you most agree with. If you do not agree with any of them, but have your own specific opinion, then please so indicate in a brief statement. My opinion is (please check one):

I most agree with the Unknown Planet Theory: ( )
I most agree with the Hollow Earth Theory: ( )
I most agree with the North Pole Theory: ( )
I most agree with the Dispersion Theory: ( )
I have an opinion that is not listed above. It is:_____
_____
_____
_____

(Optional:) Please state your reasons for believing in the possibility of any one of the above mentioned theories:
Theory: _____.
Reasons: _____
_____
_____
_____.

I am a male (   ); female (   ).
I am (age):

10-20 (   ),   21-30 (   ),   31-40 (   ),   41-50 (   ),

51-60 (   ),   61-70(   ),   71 or above (   ).

Selected Bibliography

Anderson, James H., *God's Covenant Race*, Deseret News Press, Salt Lake City, Utah.1938.383 pages.

Anderson, James H., *The Present Time & Prophecy*. Deseret News Press. Salt Lake City, Utah. 1933. 178 pages.

Book of Mormon, The. A Scripture of The Church of Jesus Christ of Latter-day Saints, Salt Lake City, Utah. 1968 edition. 568 pages.

Brough, R. Clayton, Independent Research Monographs: *The Results of a Survey of Latter-day Saint Opinion on the Present Possible Whereabouts of the Lost Ten Tribes of Israel* (1978, 9 pages); *The Hollow Earth Theory* (1975, 6 pages). Provo and Springville, Utah. Originals of both papers and notes are in the possession of the author of this book.

Brough, R. Clayton, *They Who Tarry*, Horizon Publishers, Bountiful. Utah. 1976. 98 pages.

Church News. News of The Church of Jesus Christ of Latter-day Saints. A section of the Deseret News: a daily newspaper issued from Salt Lake City, Utah. 1943-1978.

Conference Reports. Annual and Semi-annual conference speeches reports of the General Authorities of The Church of Jesus Christ of Latter-day Saints, Salt Lake City, Utah. 1897-1978.

Crowther, Duane S., *Prophecy, Key to the Future,* Horizon Publishers, Bountiful, Utah. 1962. 355 pages.

Crowther, Duane S., *Prophetic Warnings to Modern America*, Horizon Publishers, Bountiful, Utah. 1977. 415 pages.

Crowther, Duane S., *Prophets & Prophecies of the Old Testament,* Horizon Publishers, Bountiful, Utah. 1966. 644 pages.

Dalton, Matthew W., *The Period of God's Work on This Planet (or, How Science Agrees With The Revelations of Our Beloved Redeemer): A Key to This Earth*, Utah. 1906. 96 pages.

Department of Seminaries & Institutes of Religion, *Seminary Course of Study, Old Testament Student Manual*, The Church of Jesus Christ of Latter-day Saints, Salt Lake City, Utah. 1967. 96 pages.

Deseret News. A daily newspaper. issued from Salt Lake City, Utah. Particularly the editions from the years 1900-1978.

Doctrine and Covenants, The. A Scripture of The Church of Jesus Christ of Latter-day Saints, Salt Lake City, Utah. 1968 edition. 312 pages.

Ensign, The. A monthly magazine of The Church of Jesus Christ of Latter-day Saints, Salt Lake City, Utah. 1970-1978.

First Presidency of The Church of Jesus Christ of Latter-day Saints, The. *Gospel DoctrineSelections from the Sermons and Writings of Joseph F. Smith*, Deseret News Press, Salt Lake City, Utah. 1971. Volumes 1-2.

Holy Bible, The. Old and New Testaments—King James Edition. Missionary copy bound for The Church of Jesus Christ of Latter-day Saints. Salt Lake City. Utah. 1969 edition.

Improvement Era, The. A monthly magazine of The Church of Jesus Christ of Latter-day Saints. Salt Lake City, Utah. 1897-1970.

Instructor, The. A monthly magazine of The Church of Jesus Christ of Latter-day Saints, Salt Lake City, Utah. 1930-1970.

Ivins. Anthony W., *The Lost Tribes* (A personal letter on file at Brigham Young University, Provo, Utah), early 1900's. Library Number at B.Y.U.: # Mor, M238, 2 Iv 51. 15 pages.

Johnson, Benjamin F., *My Life's Review,* Zion's Printing & Publishing Company, 394 pages.

Journal History of the Church. Items about The Church of Jesus Christ of Latter-day Saints: a historical collection since the mid-1800's, available at the Church Historian's Office, Salt Lake City, Utah.

Journal of Discourses. Contains talks given by General Authorities and other Church leaders of the L.D.S. Church between the years 1851-1886 Volumes 1-26.

Juvenile Instructor. A monthly magazine of The Church of Jesus Christ of Latter-day Saints. Salt Lake City, Utah. 1866-1829.

Lindelof, O.J.S., *A Trip to the North Pole, or the Discovery of The Ten Tribes as Found in the Arctic Ocean,* Tribune Printing Company, Salt Lake City, Utah, 1903. 210 pages.

Lund, Gerald N., *The Coming of the Lord,* Bookcraft, Salt Lake City, Utah. 1971. 248 pages.

Malan, Stephen, *The Ten Tribes, Discovered & Identified,* E.A.L. Scoville Press, Salt Lake City, Utah. 1912. 170 pages.

Matthias F. Cowley, *Wilford Woodruff,* Bookcraft, Salt Lake City, Utah. 1964. 702 pages.

McAllister, Dale A., "An Analysis of Old Testament Chronology in the Light of Modern Scripture & Scientific Research," (Thesis) Brigham Young University. Utah. 1963. 119 pages.

McConkie, Bruce R., *Doctrines of Salvation: Sermons and Writings of Joseph Fielding Smith,* Bookcraft, Inc., Salt Lake City. Utah. 1954. Volumes 1-3.

McConkie, Bruce R., *Mormon Doctrine,* Bookcraft Inc., Salt Lake City, Utah. 1966. 856 pages.

Millennial Star, The. A monthly magazine of The Church of Jesus Christ of Latter-day Saints. Great Britain. 1840-1870.

New Era, The. A monthly magazine of The Church of Jesus Christ of Latter-day Saints. Salt Lake City, Utah. 1970-1978.

Newquist. Jerreld L., *Gospel Truth. Discourses and Writings of President George Q. Cannon* ,Deseret Book Company, Salt Lake City, Utah. 1957. Volumes 1-2.

Pearl of Great Price, The. A Scripture of The Church of Jesus Christ of Latter-day Saints. Salt Lake City, Utah. 1968 edition. 65 pages.

Pratt, Orson (edited by), *The Seer,* Liverpool England. 1853-1854. Volumes 1-2. 320 pages.

Pratt, Parley P., *A Voice of Warning and Instruction to all People.* Deseret News Publishing Company, Salt Lake City, Utah. 1893 (13th edition). 258 pages.

Relief Society Magazine, The. A monthly magazine of The Relief Society of The Church of Jesus Christ of Latter-day Saints. Salt Lake City, Utah. Editions particularly between 1914-1964.

Reynolds, George, *Are We of Israel?,* Deseret News Press. Salt Lake City, Utah. 1879. 136 pages.

Richards, Franklin D., & James A Little, *A Compendium of the Doctrines of the Gospel,* Deseret News, Salt Lake City. Utah. 1914. 288 pages.

Richards, Franklin D., *L.D.S. Hymns: Sacred Hymns & Spiritual Songs for The Church of Jesus Christ of Latter-day Saints.* Deseret News Company. Salt Lake City, Utah. (Eleventh Edition,1856, was published in Liverpool, England.)

Richards, LeGrand. *A Marvelous Work and A Wonder,* Deseret Book Company, Salt Lake City, Utah. 1969 edition.452 pages.

Richards, LeGrand, *Israel Do You Know,* Deseret Book Company, Salt Lake City, Utah. 1954. 254 pages.

Roberts, Brigham H., *A Comprehensive History of the Church,* Brigham Young University Press, Provo, Utah. 1956. Volumes 1-6.

Roberts, Brigham H., *Defense of the Faith and the Saints,* Deseret News, Salt Lake City, Utah. 1912. 548 pages. Volumes 1 and 2.

Skousen, W. Cleon, *Fourth Thousand Years,* Bookcraft, Salt Lake City, Utah. 1966. 846 pages.

Skousen, W. Cleon, *Prophecy and Modern Times.* Deseret Book Company, Salt Lake City, Utah. 1950. 150 pages.

Smith. Hyrum M. & Janne M Sjodahl, *Doctrine & Covenants Commentary,* Deseret Book Company, Salt Lake City, Utah. 1974. 902 pages.

Smith, Joseph, *(The Documentary) History of the Church,* Deseret Book Company. Salt Lake City, Utah.1946-1951 Volumes 1-7.

Smith, Joseph F., *Gospel Doctrine,* Deseret Book Company. Salt Lake City, Utah. 1919. 553 pages.

Smith, Joseph Fielding, *Answers to Gospel Questions,* Deseret Book Company. Salt Lake City, Utah. 1957, Volumes 1-6.

Smith, Joseph Fielding, *Church History and Modern Revelation,* a Melchizedek Priesthood Course of Study, Published by the Council of the Twelve Apostles of The Church of Jesus Christ of Latter-day Saints, Salt Lake City, Utah. 1948. Volumes 1 and 2.

Smith, Joseph Fielding, *Doctrines of Salvation, Sermons and Writings of Joseph Fielding Smith* (compiled by Bruce R. McConkie), Bookcraft Inc., Salt Lake City, Utah. 1973 Edition. Volumes 1-3.

Smith, Joseph Fielding, *Essentials in Church History,* Deseret Book Company. Salt Lake City, Utah. 1969. 648 pages.

Smith, Joseph Fielding, *The Way to Perfection, Short Discourses on Gospel Themes,* Genealogical Society of Utah. Salt Lake City, Utah. 1949 (8th edition) 364 pages. (See also 3rd edition: 1940, 365 pages.)

Smith, Robert W., *Scriptural and Secular Prophecies Pertaining to the Last Days,* Pyramid Press, Salt Lake City, Utah. 1948 (10th edition). 296 pages.

Strong, Leon M., *Three Timely Treasures,* Zion's Printing & Publishing Company, Independence, Missouri. 1949. 103 pages.

Talmage, James E, *Jesus The Christ,* Deseret Book Company, Salt Lake City, Utah. 1961 edition. 804 pages.

Talmage, James E., *The Articles of Faith,* Deseret Book Company, Salt Lake City, Utah. 1961 edition. 536 pages.

Whipple, Walt, *A Discussion of the Many Theories Concerning the Whereabouts of the Lost Ten Tribes.* A research paper prepared at Brigham Young University, Provo, Utah, 1958-1959. B.Y.U. Library, Reference #: Mormon, M238.4. W571. 35 pages.

Whitehead, Earnest L., *The House of Israel,* Zions Printing & Publishing Company, Independence, Missouri. 1947. 590 pages.

Whitney, Orson F., *Saturday Night Thoughts; A Series of Dissertations on Spiritual, Historical and Philosophic Themes,* Deseret News. Salt Lake City, Utah. 1921. 323 pages.

Widtsoe, John A., *Discourses of Brigham Young,* Deseret Book Company, Salt Lake City, Utah. 1954. 497 pages.

Index

A

Abraham, the promises the Lord made to, and his descendants, 16-17.
Anderson, Edward H., 58-61.
Anderson, James H., 55, was "father" of the Dispersion Theory, 80-86.
Anderson, Nephi, 60-61.
Apocrypha, about, 26 (footnote #10).
Arsareth, means "another land" in Hebrew, 26 (footnote #9); possible route of Ten Tribes from Palestine to, 36 (map); Ten Tribes travel through, and are lost to mankind, 28-29.
Asher, tribe of, 11-22.
Assyrians, captivity of Ten Tribes by, 23-25; Ten Tribes escape captivity 25-27.

B

Battle Of Armageddon, 96-97, 105-106.
Benjamin, tribe of, 11-22.
Bennett, Floyd, 73.
Bermuda Triangle, 73.
Biblical Choronology, 11 (footnote).
Bigfoot, 73.
Brough, R. Clayton, 30, 42, 49-50, 53-54, 61-61, 72-74.
Brown, Homer M., & Benjamin, 46-48.
Byrd, Richard, 73.

C

Canaan, establishment of Twelve Tribes in, 22 (map); later called Palestine, 17, size of, 17-18.
City Of Enoch, taken away from this earth, 43-44; where located at present time, 43 (footnote).
City Of Zion, see "New Jerusalem."
ConcaveTheory, see "Hollow Earth Theory."
Cowdery, Oliver, 62.
Cowley, Matthias, 45.
Crowther, Duane S., 19, 87-89, 92, 94-96.

D

Dalton, Matthew W., 50-53.
Dan, tribe of, 11-22.
Dibble, Philo, 50-52.
Dibble, Sidney, 51-53.
Dispersion Theory, 42, directly conflicts with the teachings of past and present General Authorities, 73-74; explained 73-88.

E

Egypt, number of Israelites who exited from, with Moses, 16-17.
Endowments, children of Ephraim will assist in giving, to the Lost Ten Tribes when they return in the Last Days, 103.
Ephraim, tribe of, 14-16; why so many patriarchal blessings inform people they are from the tribe of, 32-35.
Events, which will precede the return of the Lost Ten Tribes in the Last Days, 92-95.

G

Gad, tribe of, 11-22.
Gentiles, time of, will be fulfilled before Lost Ten Tribes return in Last Days, 92-94.
Grant, Heber J., 80.

H

History, of the Twelve Tribes of Israel, 11-22; the geography and, of the Lost Ten Tribes, 23-36.
Hollow Earth (or Concave) Theory, 42, explained, 53-61.

I

Isaac, Promises the Lord made with, 12-14.
Israelites, not all who traveled northward remained with the Lost Ten Tribes, 30-35; who they are, 13-14.
Issachar, tribe of, 11-22.
Ivins, Anthony W., 14, 17, 20-21, 31, 81-83.

J

Phelps, William W, 62.
Pratt, Orson, 43, 48, 53-54, 63-64, 92-98, 100-107;
Pratt, Parley P., 31, 49-50.
Prophecies, regarding the return of the Lost Ten Tribes in the Last Days, 92-107.

R

Records, of the Lost Ten Tribes, 29-30, 85-86, 101-102.
Reuben, tribe of, 11-22.
Reynolds, George, 27-29, 32-35, 64, 83-84.
Richards, Franklin D.,30, 44, 91.
Richards, Legrand,13-14, 31.
Roberts, Brigham H., 31, 49, 74-77.

S

Scriptures, of the Lost Ten Tribes, 29-30, 85-86, 101-102.
Simeon, tribe of, 11-22.
Sjodahl, Janne M., 71-72.
Skousen, W. Cleon, 23-25, 32-35, 92, 90-91.
Smith, Hyrum M., 71-72.
Smith, Joseph, 30, location of the Lost Ten Tribes—see various theories discussed in this book and those statements which were attributed to him by other individuals, 37-91 received D&C sections 133 and 110 containing information about the Lost Ten Tribes, 41.
Smith, Joseph Fielding, 30-32, 95, 105.
Smith, Robert W., 48.
Snow, Eliza R., wrote a song as to the location of the Lost Ten Tribes, 43-45.
Song, a, as to the location of the Lost Ten Tribes, 43-45.
Strong, Leon M, 45.
Survey, example of a L.D.S., sheet, concerning the present possible whereabouts of the Lost Ten Tribes of Israel, 108-109; results of a L.D.S., on the present possible whereabouts of the Lost Ten Tribes of Israel, 42 (footnote).
Symmes Hole Theory, 55-58.
Symmes, John C., 55-58.

T

Talmage, James E., 31, 34-35, 85, 102.
Ten Tribes, see "Lost Ten Tribes."
Theories, as to the location of the Lost Ten Tribes, 37-91; early proposed by biblical and secular historians as to the location of the Lost Ten Tribes, 39-40; major, proposed by Latter-day Saints to explain the present whereabouts of the Lost Ten Tribes, 41-42; summary of the various, 90-91.
Tiede, Tom, 58.
Twelve Thousand High Priests, will go forth to all nations in the Last Days to preach the gospel,103-104.
Twelve Tribes Of Israel, history of, 11-22; in the land of Canaan, 16-18; map of, 22.

U

U.F.O.'s, 73.
Unknown Planet Theory, 42, explained, 42-49.
U.S.S. Nautilus, 73.

V

Volcanos, see "Hollow Earth Theory."

W

Whipple, Walt, 40-43, 45, 50, 70, 78, 80, 87, 89.
Whitehead, Earnest L., 26, 29, 86-87.
Whitney, Orson F., 31-32.
Woodruff, Wilford, 45, 49, 85, 99, 103.

Y

Young, Brigham, 45, 81-82.

Z

Zebulun, tribe of, 11-22.
Zion, an area encompassing the city of the New Jerusalem 96; how long will the Lost Ten Tribes reside in, when they return,103-104; Lost Ten Tribes will come to, in Last Days, 95-107.

About the Author

Robert Clayton Brough, a native Californian, moved to Utah in 1971 to attend Brigham Young University, where he received his B.S. degree in 1974 and his M.S. degree in 1975, both in geography. He presently teaches this subject at Eisenhower Junior High School and is a weather forecaster for KTVX-TV in Salt Lake CIty, Utah.

Elder Brough has lectured extensively and written several books and articles on geography, history, climatology and atmospheric phenomena. He is also the author of five other books dealing with LDS theology: *His Servants Speak—Statements by Latter-day Saint Leaders on Contemporary Topics; They Who Tarry—The Doctrine of Translated Beings; Our First Estate—The Doctrine of Man's Pre-mortal existence; Understanding Patriarchal Blessings,* and *Scientific Support for Scriptural Stories.*

As a youth, Elder Brough took active part in Church activities and scouting, and participated in track and field sports. His LDS Church experience includes completion of a full-time mission to the Eastern States, and service as a stake missionary, scoutmaster, genealogist, gospel doctrine teacher, in-service instructor, bishop's counselor and high councilman.